Solicitors' Accounts Manual

11TH EDITION

Solicitors' Accounts Manual

11TH EDITION

Crown copyright material in Annexes A and D is reproduced with the permission of the Controller of Her Majesty's Stationery Office

1st edition 1986
2nd edition 1987
3rd edition 1990
4th edition 1992
5th edition 1994
6th edition 1996
7th edition 1999
8th edition 2001
9th edition 2004
10th edition 2008

This 11th edition published in 2009 by the Law Society
113 Chancery Lane, London WC2A 1PL

Typeset by Columns Design Ltd, Reading
Printed by TJ International Ltd, Padstow, Cornwall

FSC
Mixed Sources
Product group from well-managed
forests and other controlled sources
Cert no. SGS-COC-2482
www.fsc.org
© 1996 Forest Stewardship Council

The paper used for the text pages of this book is FSC certified.
FSC (the Forest Stewardship Council) is an international network to promote responsible management of the world's forests.

Contents

Preface

This is the 11th edition of the Solicitors' Accounts Manual. It contains a summary of the professional requirements in relation to the handling of client money.

The Solicitors' Accounts Rules 1998 (SAR) apply to practice carried on from an office in England and Wales. Rules 15.15, 15.27 and 20.08 of the Solicitors' Code of Conduct 2007 (the Code) apply to practice carried on from an office outside England and Wales.

Practice in England and Wales

The SAR are contained in Part 1 and include all changes made to the rules since publication of the tenth edition of the Manual up to 31 March 2009.

Residual client account balances

From 14 July 2008, a new rule 15(3) introduces a specific obligation to return client money promptly, once there is no longer any proper reason to retain the funds. A new rule 15(4) requires solicitors to report to clients if funds need to be retained, and to report on an annual basis for as long as those funds are retained. These new duties do not have retrospective effect and apply only to client funds received and held on or after 14 July 2008.

Rule 22 has been amended to permit solicitors to withdraw from client account residual balances of £50 or less without prior authorisation from the Solicitors Regulation Authority (SRA), subject to paying the balances to a charity and complying with the other safeguards set out in a new rule 22(2A). An indemnity from the charity concerned is not a requirement. Solicitors are able to use the new procedure to deal with historic small balances which existed prior to the new provisions taking effect, as well as those residual balances which arise on or after 14 July 2008.

Prior SRA authorisation is still required for amounts exceeding £50, or where the money represents the solicitor's costs (note (viiia) to rule 22). SRA authorisation may still be sought where the balance is £50 or less if that is preferred.

Under new paragraphs 4.6 and 4.7 of the Guidelines for Accounting Procedures and Systems at Appendix 3 to the SAR, solicitors should establish policies and systems for the timely closure of files and prompt accounting for surplus balances, and for reporting to clients when funds are retained.

Note (iv) to rule 42 and rule 44 have been amended to clarify that the reporting accountant needs to check the procedural side only of the rule 22(2A) requirements. The reporting accountant will report on compliance with rules 15(3)–(4), and on any substantial departures from the new Guidelines, in the usual way.

Legal disciplinary practices and firm-based regulation

With effect from 31 March 2009, changes have been made throughout the SAR to reflect the introduction of legal disciplinary practices and firm-based regulation under the Legal Services Act 2007 (the Act).

Practices may include non-solicitor lawyers as managers (partners in a partnership, members of an LLP or directors of a company), and up to 25 per cent of managers who are not legally qualified. The rules apply to all types of practice (sole practice, partnerships, LLPs and companies), and to the individual managers and employees.

Partnerships are governed by the rules as, in common with LLPs and companies, they must now be recognised by the SRA and are regulated as recognised bodies by the SRA.

Non-solicitor lawyers include barristers, notaries, legal executives, licensed conveyancers, patent agents, trade mark agents and costs draftsmen (rule 2(2) (ma)).

The position of solicitors who are managers or employees in firms regulated by other approved regulators, such as the Council for Licensed Conveyancers, is dealt with in rule 5(d) and note (iii) to rule 5.

All managers, whether legally qualified or not, will be permitted to authorise client account withdrawals under rule 23, but they will need to have an appropriate understanding of the requirements of the rules (paragraph 4.1A of the Guidelines for Accounting Procedures and Systems at Appendix 3 SAR). The signing criteria have also been relaxed for Fellows of the Institute of Legal Executives and licensed conveyancers.

Abolition of "controlled trust"

The Act has abolished the concept of a "controlled trust", so all money held by a practice will be either client money or office money (rule 13). The provisions for the payment of interest, or a sum in lieu of interest, on client money now also apply to money previously defined as "controlled trust money" (rule 24).

Abolition of interest certificates

The statutory basis for interest certificates has been removed. Interest complaints will be dealt with by the Legal Complaints Service (note (xa) to rule 24).

Accountants' reports

The Act enables the introduction of more flexible, risk-based provisions for the delivery of accountants' reports. The SAR retain the basic requirement for an annual report, but provide for delivery on a different basis where there are public interest concerns (rule 35).

The Act has also introduced a mandatory whistleblowing duty for reporting accountants, which is reflected in an amended rule 38. This rule previously provided for the right of reporting accountants to whistleblow but imposed no duty to do so.

Clarificatory changes

A number of clarificatory changes have also been made, with effect from 31 March 2009:

- rule 2(1) on the mandatory nature of the notes to the SAR;

- rule 15(2)(d) on using a client account for paying a sum in lieu of interest;

- note (viii) to rule 15 on the aggregation of client accounts;

- note (iii) to rule 16 and note (iia) to rule 17 on including money withheld from a client account in the monthly reconciliations;

- paragraph 2.2 of the Guidelines for Accounting Procedures and Systems on access to the on-line version of the SAR;

- paragraph 5.6 of the Guidelines on including any digital images of paid cheques in a firm's retention policies and systems.

Overseas practice

Rules 15.15 (Deposit interest), 15.27 (Accounts) and 20.08 (Production of documents and information) of the Code are specific to overseas practice as defined in rule 24 of the Code (see Part 2). (The SAR do not apply to overseas practice.)

"Overseas practice" continues to cover the practice of a solicitor or a recognised body from an office outside England and Wales; and the practice of a registered European lawyer (REL) from an office in Scotland or Northern Ireland.

Following the Legal Services Act 2007, and with effect from 31 March 2009, the definition of overseas practice has been widened to include:

- the practice from an office outside England and Wales of a manager of a recognised body who is a lawyer of England and Wales;

- the activities of an individual non-lawyer as a manager of a recognised body practising from an office outside England and Wales; and

- the activities of a body corporate as a manager of a recognised body practising from an office outside England and Wales.

A "solicitor-controlled recognised body" (in which English lawyers form the dominant, or equal largest, group of lawyers – see rule 24 of the Code) is subject to rule 15 in relation to practice from an office outside England and Wales.

An "REL-controlled recognised body" (in which RELs and English lawyers together form the dominant, or equal largest, group of lawyers – see rule 24 of the Code) is subject to rule 15 in relation to practice from an office in Scotland or Northern Ireland.

A lawyer of England and Wales, other than a solicitor, is subject to rule 15 in relation to practice as a manager of a "solicitor-controlled recognised body" from an office outside England and Wales.

A lawyer of England and Wales, other than a solicitor, is subject to rule 15 in relation to practice as a manager of an "REL-controlled recognised body" from an office in Scotland or Northern Ireland.

A European lawyer registered with the Bar Standards Board is subject to rule 15 in relation to practice as a manager of a "solicitor-controlled recognised body" or an "REL-controlled recognised body" from an office in Scotland or Northern Ireland.

A non-lawyer is subject to rule 15 in relation to practice as a manager of a "solicitor-controlled recognised body" from an office outside England and Wales.

A non-lawyer is subject to rule 15 in relation to practice as a manager of an "REL-controlled recognised body" from an office in Scotland or Northern Ireland.

A recognised body which is not a "solicitor-controlled recognised body" or an "REL-controlled recognised body" will not itself have to comply with rule 15. However, individual solicitors who are managers or employees will still be subject to rule 15 (and so will individual RELs in Scotland or Northern Ireland).

Non-lawyer employees of a recognised body or a recognised sole practitioner are not subject to rule 15 in respect of overseas practice.

Registered foreign lawyers are not subject to rule 15 in respect of overseas practice.

A single accountant's report may be submitted in relation to a practice which has offices in, and outside, England and Wales. Such a report must cover compliance with both the SAR and rule 15.27(3) of the Code.

Part 2 also contains other extracts from the Code which relate to the keeping of accounts by solicitors.

The full text of the Code can be found on the website of the Solicitors Regulation Authority at **www.sra.org.uk**. The website also contains an electronic version of the SAR.

March 2009

Part 1

Solicitors' Accounts Rules 1998

[With consolidated amendments to 31 March 2009]

Authority: *Made under sections 32, 33A, 34 and 37 of the Solicitors Act 1974 and section 9 of the Administration of Justice Act 1985 with the concurrence, where requisite, of the Master of the Rolls under those sections and of the Lord Chancellor under paragraph 16 of Schedule 22 to the Legal Services Act 2007;*

date: *22nd July 1998;*

replacing: *the Solicitors' Accounts Rules 1991, the Solicitors' Accounts (Legal Aid Temporary Provision) Rule 1992 and the Accountant's Report Rules 1991;*

regulating: *the accounts of solicitors and their employees, registered European lawyers and their employees, registered foreign lawyers, and recognised bodies and their managers and employees, in respect of practice in England and Wales.*

For the definition of words in italics see rule 2 – Interpretation.

Part A – General

Rule 1 – Principles

A *solicitor* must comply with the requirements of rule 1 of the Solicitors' Code of Conduct 2007, and in particular must:

   (a) keep other people's money separate from money belonging to the *solicitor* or the practice;

   (b) keep other people's money safely in a *bank* or *building society* account identifiable as a *client account* (except when the rules specifically provide otherwise);

   (c) use each *client's* money for that *client's* matters only;

   (d) use money held as *trustee* of a *trust* for the purposes of that *trust* only;

   (e) establish and maintain proper accounting systems, and proper internal controls over those systems, to ensure compliance with the rules;

   (f) keep proper accounting records to show accurately the position with regard to the money held for each *client* and *trust*;

   (g) account for interest on other people's money in accordance with the rules;

(h)   co-operate with the *SRA* in checking compliance with the rules; and

(i)   deliver annual accountant's reports as required by the rules.

Rule 2 – Interpretation

(1)   The notes form part of the rules and are mandatory.

(2)   In the rules, unless the context otherwise requires:

(a)   "accounting period" has the meaning given in rule 36;

(b)   "agreed fee" has the meaning given in rule 19(5);

(ba) "approved regulator" means any body listed as an approved regulator in paragraph 1 of Schedule 4 to the Legal Services Act 2007 (whether or not that paragraph has been brought into force), or designated as an approved regulator by an order under paragraph 17 of that Schedule;

(bb) "authorised non-SRA firm" means a *firm* which is not authorised to practise by the *SRA* but is authorised to practise by another *approved regulator*;

(c)   "bank" has the meaning given in section 87(1) of the Solicitors Act 1974;

(d)   "building society" means a building society within the meaning of the Building Societies Act 1986;

(e)   "client" means the person for whom a *solicitor* acts;

(f)   "client account" has the meaning given in rule 14(2);

(g)   "client money" has the meaning given in rule 13;

(h)   [deleted]

(i)   [deleted]

(j)   "costs" means a *solicitor's fees* and *disbursements*;

(ja) "Court of Protection deputy" includes a deputy who was appointed by the Court of Protection as a receiver under the Mental Health Act 1983 before the commencement day of the Mental Capacity Act 2005;

(k)   "disbursement" means any sum spent or to be spent by a *solicitor* on behalf of the *client* or *trust* (including any VAT element);

(l)   "fees" of a *solicitor* means the *solicitor's* own charges or profit costs (including any VAT element);

(la) "firm" means a sole practitioner, *partnership*, *LLP* or company operating as a legal practice;

(m)   "general client account" has the meaning given in rule 14(5)(b);

(ma) "lawyer" includes a barrister, notary, legal executive, licensed conveyancer, patent agent, trade mark agent or costs draftsman;

(mb) "LLP" means a limited liability partnership incorporated under the Limited Liability Partnerships Act 2000;

(mc) "manager" means:

(i)   a *partner* in a *partnership*;

(ii)   a member of an *LLP*; or

(iii) a director of a company;

(n)   "mixed payment" has the meaning given in rule 20(1);

(o)   "non-solicitor employer" means any employer other than a *solicitor* or *authorised non-SRA firm*;

(p)   "office account" means an account of the *solicitor* or the practice for holding *office money*, or other means of holding *office money* (for example, the office cash box);

(q)   "office money" has the meaning given in rule 13;

(qa) "partner" means a person who is or is held out as a partner in an unincorporated practice;

(qb) "partnership" means an unincorporated partnership, and includes any unincorporated practice in which persons are or are held out as partners, but does not include an *LLP*;

(r)   "principal" means:

(i)   a sole practitioner;

(ii)   a *partner* in a *partnership*;

(iia) in the case of a *recognised body* which is an *LLP* or company, the *recognised body* itself;

(iii) the principal *solicitor of the Supreme Court* or *registered European lawyer* (or any one of them) employed by a *non-solicitor employer* (for example, in a law centre or in commerce and industry);

(s)   "professional disbursement" means the fees of counsel or other lawyer, or of a professional or other agent or expert instructed by the *solicitor*;

(t)   "recognised body" means a *partnership*, company or *LLP* recognised by the *SRA* under section 9 of the Administration of Justice Act 1985;

(ta) "recognised sole practitioner" means a *solicitor of the Supreme Court* or *registered European lawyer* authorised by the *SRA* under section 1B of the Solicitors Act 1974 to practise as a sole practitioner;

(tb) "registered European lawyer" means a person registered by the *SRA* under regulation 17 of the European Communities (Lawyer's Practice) Regulations 2000;

(u)   "registered foreign lawyer" means a person registered by the *SRA* under section 89 of the Courts and Legal Services Act 1990;

(ua) "regular payment" has the meaning given in rule 21;

(v)   "separate designated client account" has the meaning given in rule 14(5)(a);

(w) [deleted]

(x) "solicitor" means:

    (i)   a *solicitor of the Supreme Court*;

    (ii)   a *registered European lawyer*;

    (iii)   a *registered foreign lawyer* practising:

        (A)   as a *partner* in a *partnership* which is a *recognised body* or *authorised non-SRA firm*; or in a *partnership* which should be a *recognised body* but has not been recognised by the *SRA*;

        (B)   as the director of a company which is a *recognised body* or *authorised non-SRA firm*, or as the director of a company which is a *manager* of a *recognised body* or *authorised non-SRA firm*;

        (C)   as a member of an *LLP* which is a *recognised body* or *authorised non-SRA firm*, or as a member of an *LLP* which is a *manager* of a *recognised body* or *authorised non-SRA firm*;

        (D)   as a *partner* in a *partnership* with separate legal personality which is a *manager* of a *recognised body* or *authorised non-SRA firm*;

        (E)   as an employee of a *recognised body* or *recognised sole practitioner*; or

        (F)   as an employee of a *partnership* which should be a *recognised body* but has not been authorised by the *SRA*, or of a sole practitioner who should be a *recognised sole practitioner* but has not been authorised by the *SRA*;

    (iv)   a *recognised body*;

    (v)   a *manager* of a *recognised* body;

    (vi)   an employee of a *recognised body* or *recognised sole practitioner*; or

    (vii)   an employee of a *partnership* which should be a *recognised body* but has not been authorised by the *SRA*, or of a sole practitioner who should be a *recognised sole practitioner* but has not been authorised by the *SRA*;

(xa) "solicitor-manager", in rule 22(8)(b), means a *solicitor of the Supreme Court* (or *registered European lawyer*) appointed by the personal representatives of a deceased sole practitioner to carry on the practice;

(xb) "solicitor of the Supreme Court" means an individual who is a solicitor of the Supreme Court of England and Wales; and, with effect from the coming into force of section 59(1) of the Constitutional Reform Act 2005, all references to a solicitor of the Supreme Court are to be replaced by references to a solicitor of the Senior Courts;

(xc) "SRA" means the Solicitors Regulation Authority, and reference to the SRA as an *approved regulator* means the SRA carrying out regulatory functions assigned to the Law Society as an *approved regulator*;

(y) "trustee" includes a personal representative (i.e. an executor or an administrator), and "trust" includes the duties of a personal representative;

(z) "without delay" means, in normal circumstances, either on the day of receipt or on the next working day; and

(za) the singular includes the plural and vice versa, and references to the masculine or feminine include the neuter.

Notes

(i) Although many of the rules are expressed as applying to an individual solicitor, the effect of the definition of "solicitor" in rule 2(2)(x) is that the rules apply equally to all those who carry on or work in a practice and to the practice itself. See also rule 4 (persons governed by the rules) and rule 5 (persons exempt from the rules). Note however that, until 1 July 2009, rules which are stated to apply to a recognised sole practitioner, or the employee of a recognised sole practitioner, will apply to a sole practitioner or the employee of a sole practitioner.

(ii) A client account must be at a bank or building society's branch in England and Wales – see rule 14(4).

(iii) For the full definition of a "European authorised institution" (rule 2(2)(c)), see the Banking Co-ordination (Second Council Directive) Regulations 1992 (S.I. 1992 no. 3218).

(iv) [deleted]

(v) The fees of interpreters, translators, process servers, surveyors, estate agents, etc., instructed by the solicitor are professional disbursements (see rule 2(2) (s)). Travel agents' charges are not professional disbursements.

(vi) The general definition of "office account" is wide (see rule 2(2)(p)). However, rule 19(1)(b) (receipt and transfer of costs) and rule 21(1)(b) and 21(2)(b) (payments from the Legal Services Commission) specify that certain money is to be placed in an office account at a bank or building society.

(vii) An index is attached to the rules but it does not form part of the rules. For the status of the flowchart (Appendix 1) and the chart dealing with special situations (Appendix 2), see note (xiii) to rule 13.

Rule 3 – Geographical scope

The rules apply to practice carried on from an office in England and Wales.

Note

Accounts of a practice carried on from an office outside England and Wales are governed by the Solicitors' Code of Conduct 2007 rule 15.27 (accounts), rule 15.15 (deposit interest) and rule 20.08 (production of documents and information).

Rule 4 – Persons governed by the rules

(1) The rules apply to:

    (a) *solicitors of the Supreme Court* or *registered European lawyers* who are:

        (i) sole practitioners;

        (ii) *partners* in a *partnership* which is a *recognised body* or *authorised non-SRA firm*, or in a *partnership* which should be a *recognised body* but has not been recognised by the *SRA*;

        (iii) assistants, associates, professional support lawyers, consultants, locums or persons otherwise employed in the practice of a *recognised body*, *recognised sole practitioner* or *authorised non-SRA firm*; or of a *partnership* which should be a *recognised body* but has not been recognised by the *SRA*, or of a sole practitioner who should be a *recognised sole practitioner* but has not been authorised by the *SRA*;

        (iv) employed as in-house lawyers by a *non-solicitor employer* (for example, in a law centre or in commerce and industry);

        (v) directors of companies which are *recognised bodies* or *authorised non-SRA firms*, or of companies which are *managers* of *recognised bodies* or *authorised non-SRA firms*;

        (vi) members of *LLPs* which are *recognised bodies* or *authorised non-SRA firms*, or of *LLPs* which are *managers* of *recognised bodies* or *authorised non-SRA firms*; or

        (vii) *partners* in a *partnership* with separate legal personality which is a *manager* of a *recognised body* or *authorised non-SRA firm*;

    (b) *registered foreign lawyers* who are practising in any of the ways set out in rule 2(2)(x)(iii);

    (c) *recognised bodies*;

    (d) *managers* and employees of a *recognised body*, or of a *partnership* which should be a *recognised body* but has not been authorised by the *SRA*; and

    (e) employees of a *recognised sole practitioner*, or of a sole practitioner who should be a *recognised sole practitioner* but has not been authorised by the *SRA*.

(2) Part F of the rules (accountants' reports) also applies to reporting accountants.

Notes

(i)   All employees of a recognised body are directly subject to the rules, following the amendment of section 9 of the Administration of Justice Act 1985 by the Legal Services Act 2007. All employees of a recognised sole practitioner are also directly subject to the rules as from the coming into force of new sections 1B and 34A of the Solicitors Act 1974. Non-compliance by any member of staff will also lead to the principals being in breach of the rules – see rule 6. Misconduct by an employee can also lead to an order of the SRA or the Solicitors Disciplinary Tribunal under section 43 of the Solicitors Act 1974 imposing restrictions on his or her employment.

(ii)   Solicitors who have held or received client money, but no longer do so, whether or not they continue in practice, continue to be bound by some of the rules – for instance:

- rule 7 (duty to remedy breaches);

- rule 19(2), and note (xi) to rule 19, rule 32(8) to (15) and rule 33 (retention of records);

- rule 34 (production of records);

- Part F (accountants' reports), and in particular rule 35 and rule 36(5) (delivery of final report), and rule 38(2) and rule 46 (completion of checklist).

(iii) The rules do not cover a solicitor's trusteeships carried on in a purely personal capacity outside any legal practice. It will normally be clear from the terms of the appointment whether the solicitor is being appointed trustee in a purely personal capacity or in his or her professional capacity. If a solicitor is charging for the work, it is clearly being done as solicitor. Use of professional stationery may also indicate that the work is being done in a professional capacity.

(iv)   A solicitor who wishes to retire from private practice must make a decision about any professional trusteeship. There are three possibilities:

(a)   continue to act as a professional trustee (as evidenced by, for instance, charging for work done, or by continuing to use the title "solicitor" in connection with the trust). In this case, the solicitor must continue to hold a practising certificate, and money subject to the trust must continue to be dealt with in accordance with the rules.

(b)   continue to act as trustee, but in a purely personal capacity. In this case, the solicitor must stop charging for the work, and must not be held out as a solicitor (unless this is qualified by words such as "non-practising" or "retired") in connection with the trust.

(c)   cease to be a trustee.

Rule 5 – Persons exempt from the rules

The rules do not apply to:

(a) a *solicitor* when practising as an employee of:

   (i)   a local authority;

   (ii)   statutory undertakers;

   (iii) a body whose accounts are audited by the Comptroller and Auditor General;

   (iv)   the Duchy of Lancaster;

   (v)   the Duchy of Cornwall; or

   (vi)   the Church Commissioners; or

(b) a *solicitor* who practises as the Solicitor of the City of London; or

(c) a *solicitor* when carrying out the functions of:

   (i)   a coroner or other judicial office; or

   (ii)   a sheriff or under-sheriff; or

(d) a *solicitor* when practising as a *manager* or employee of an *authorised non-SRA firm* and acting within the scope of that *firm's* authorisation to practise.

Notes

(i)   "Statutory undertakers" means:

   (a) any persons authorised by any enactment to carry on any railway, light railway, tramway, road transport, water transport, canal, inland navigation, dock, harbour, pier or lighthouse undertaking or any undertaking for the supply of hydraulic power; and

   (b) any licence holder within the meaning of the Electricity Act 1989, any public gas supplier, any water or sewerage undertaker, the Environment Agency, any public telecommunications operator, the Post Office, the Civil Aviation Authority and any relevant airport operator within the meaning of Part V of the Airports Act 1986.

(ii) "Local authority" means any of those bodies which are listed in section 270 of the Local Government Act 1972 or in section 21(1) of the Local Government and Housing Act 1989.

(iii) A solicitor practising as a manager or employee of an authorised non-SRA firm is exempt from the Solicitors' Accounts Rules when the solicitor is acting within the scope of the firm's authorisation. Thus if a solicitor is a partner or employee in a firm authorised by the Council for Licensed Conveyancers, the rules will not apply to any money received by the solicitor in connection with conveyancing work. However if the solicitor does in-house litigation work – say collecting money owed to the firm – the Solicitors' Accounts Rules will apply to any money received by the solicitor in that context. This is because, whilst in-house litigation work is within the scope of the solicitor's authorisation as an individual, it is outside the scope of authorisation of the firm.

Rule 6 – Principals' responsibility for compliance

All the *principals* in a practice must ensure compliance with the rules by the *principals* themselves and by everyone employed in the practice. This duty also extends to the directors of a *recognised body* which is a company, or to the members of a *recognised body* which is an *LLP*.

Rule 7 – Duty to remedy breaches

(1)   Any breach of the rules must be remedied promptly upon discovery. This includes the replacement of any money improperly withheld or withdrawn from a *client account*.

(2)   In a private practice, the duty to remedy breaches rests not only on the person causing the breach, but also on all the *principals* in the practice. This duty extends to replacing missing *client money* from the *principals'* own resources, even if the money has been misappropriated by an employee or another *principal*, and whether or not a claim is subsequently made on the Solicitors' Indemnity or Compensation Funds or on the *firm's* insurance.

Note

For payment of interest when money should have been held in a client account but was not, see rule 24(2).

Rule 8 – [repealed]

Rule 9 – Liquidators, trustees in bankruptcy, Court of Protection deputies and trustees of occupational pension schemes

(1)   A *solicitor* who in the course of practice acts as

- a liquidator,

- a trustee in bankruptcy,

- a *Court of Protection deputy*, or

- a trustee of an occupational pension scheme which is subject to section 47(1)(a) of the Pensions Act 1995 (appointment of an auditor) **and** section 49(1) (separate bank account) **and** regulations under section 49(2)(b) (books and records), must comply with:

(a)   the appropriate statutory rules or regulations;

(b)   the principles set out in rule 1; and

(c)   the requirements of paragraphs (2) to (4) below;

and will then be deemed to have satisfactorily complied with the Solicitors' Accounts Rules.

(2)   In respect of any records kept under the appropriate statutory rules, there must also be compliance with:

(a)   rule 32(8) – bills and notifications of costs;

(b)   rule 32(9)(c) – retention of records;

(c)   rule 32(12) – centrally kept records;

(d)   rule 34 – production of records; and

(e)   rule 42(1)(l) and (p) – reporting accountant to check compliance.

(3)   If a liquidator or trustee in bankruptcy uses any of the practice's *client accounts* for holding money pending transfer to the Insolvency Services Account or to a local bank account authorised by the Secretary of State, he or she must comply with the Solicitors' Accounts Rules in all respects whilst the money is held in the *client account.*

(4)   If the appropriate statutory rules or regulations do not govern the holding or receipt of *client money* in a particular situation (for example, money below a certain limit), the *solicitor* must comply with the Solicitors' Accounts Rules in all respects in relation to that money.

Notes

(i)   The Insolvency Regulations 1994 (S.I. 1994 no. 2507) regulate liquidators and trustees in bankruptcy.

(ii)   The Court of Protection Rules 2007 (S.I. 2007 no. 1744 (L.12)) regulate Court of Protection deputies (see rule 2(2)(ja)).

(iii) Money held or received by solicitor liquidators, trustees in bankruptcy, Court of Protection deputies and trustees of occupational pension schemes is client money but, because of the statutory rules and rule 9(1), it will not normally be kept in a client account. If for any reason it is held in a client account, the Solicitors' Accounts Rules apply to that money for the time it is so held (see rule 9(3) and (4)).

Rule 10 – Joint accounts

(1) If a *solicitor* acting in a *client's* matter holds or receives money jointly with the *client*, another *solicitors'* practice or another third party, the rules in general do not apply, but the following must be complied with:

(a) rule 32(8) – bills and notifications of costs;

(b) rule 32(9)(b)(ii) – retention of statements and passbooks;

(c) rule 32(13) – centrally kept records;

(d) rule 34 – production of records; and

(e) rule 42(1)(m) and (p) – reporting accountant to check compliance.

Operation of the joint account by the solicitor only

(2) If the joint account is operated only by the *solicitor*, the *solicitor* must ensure that he or she receives the statements from the *bank*, *building society* or other financial institution, and has possession of any passbooks.

Shared operation of the joint account

(3) If the *solicitor* shares the operation of the joint account with the *client*, another *solicitor's* practice or another third party, the *solicitor* must:

(a) ensure that he or she receives the statements or duplicate statements from the *bank*, *building society* or other financial institution and retains them in accordance with rule 32(9)(b)(ii); and

(b) ensure that he or she either has possession of any passbooks, or takes copies of the passbook entries before handing any passbook to the other signatory, and retains them in accordance with rule 32(9)(b)(ii).

Operation of the joint account by the other account holder

(4) If the joint account is operated solely by the other account holder, the *solicitor* must ensure that he or she receives the statements or duplicate statements from the *bank*, *building society* or other financial institution and retains them in accordance with rule 32(9)(b)(ii).

Note

Although a joint account is not a client account, money held in a joint account is client money.

Rule 11 – Operation of a client's own account

(1) If a *solicitor* in the course of practice operates a *client's* own account as signatory (for example, as donee under a power of attorney), the rules in general do not apply, but the following must be complied with:

(a) rule 33(1) to (3) – accounting records for clients' own accounts;

(b) rule 34 – production of records; and

(c) rule 42(1)(n) and (p) – reporting accountant to check compliance.

Operation by the solicitor only

(2) If the account is operated by the *solicitor* only, the *solicitor* must ensure that he or she receives the statements from the *bank, building society* or other financial institution, and has possession of any passbooks.

Shared operation of the account

(3) If the *solicitor* shares the operation of the account with the *client* or a co-attorney outside the *solicitor's* practice, the *solicitor* must:

(a) ensure that he or she receives the statements or duplicate statements from the *bank, building society* or other financial institution and retains them in accordance with rule 33(1) to (3); and

(b) ensure that he or she either has possession of any passbooks, or takes copies of the passbook entries before handing any passbook to the *client* or co-attorney, and retains them in accordance with rule 33(1) to (3).

Operation of the account for a limited purpose

(4) If the *solicitor* is given authority (whether as attorney or otherwise) to operate the account for a limited purpose only, such as the taking up of a share rights issue during the *client's* temporary absence, the *solicitor* need not receive statements or possess passbooks, provided that he or she retains details of all cheques drawn or paid in, and retains copies of all passbook entries, relating to the transaction, and retains them in accordance with rule 33(1) and (2).

Application

(5) This rule applies only to *solicitors* in private practice.

Notes

(i) Money held in a client's own account (under a power of attorney or otherwise) is not "client money" for the purpose of the rules because it is not "held or received" by the solicitor. If the solicitor closes the account and receives the closing balance, this becomes client money and must be paid into a client account, unless the client instructs to the contrary in accordance with rule 16(1)(a).

(ii) A solicitor who merely pays money into a client's own account, or helps the client to complete forms in relation to such an account, is not "operating" the account.

(iii)   A solicitor executor who operates the deceased's account (whether before or after the grant of probate) will be subject to the limited requirements of rule 11. If the account is subsequently transferred into the solicitor's name, or a new account is opened in the solicitor's name, the solicitor will have "held or received" client money and is then subject to all the rules.

(iv)   The rules do not cover money held or received by a solicitor attorney acting in a purely personal capacity outside any legal practice. If a solicitor is charging for the work, it is clearly being done in the course of legal practice. See rule 4, note (iv) for the choices which can be made on retirement from private practice.

(v)   "A client's own account" covers all accounts in a client's own name, whether opened by the client himself or herself, or by the solicitor on the client's instructions under rule 16(1)(b).

(vi)   "A client's own account" also includes an account opened in the name of a person designated by the client under rule 16(1)(b).

(vii) Solicitors should also remember the requirements of rule 32(8) – bills and notifications of costs.

(viii) For payment of interest, see rule 24, note (iii).

Rule 12 – Solicitor's rights not affected

Nothing in these rules deprives a *solicitor* of any recourse or right, whether by way of lien, set off, counterclaim, charge or otherwise, against money standing to the credit of a *client account*.

Rule 13 – Categories of money

All money held or received in the course of practice falls into one or other of the following categories:

(a)   "client money" – money held or received for a *client* or as *trustee*, and all other money which is not *office money*; or

(b)   "office money" – money which belongs to the *solicitor* or the practice.

Notes

(i)   "Client money" includes money held or received:

       (aa) as trustee;

       (a) as agent, bailee, stakeholder, or as the donee of a power of attorney, or as a liquidator, trustee in bankruptcy, Court of Protection deputy or trustee of an occupational pension scheme;

(b) for payment of unpaid professional disbursements (for definition of "professional disbursement" see rule 2(2)(s));

(c) for payment of stamp duty land tax, Land Registry registration fees, telegraphic transfer fees and court fees; this is not office money because the solicitor has not incurred an obligation to the Inland Revenue, the Land Registry, the bank or the court to pay the duty or fee (contrast with note (xi)(c)(C) below); (on the other hand, if the solicitor has already paid the duty or fee out of his or her own resources, or has received the service on credit, payment subsequently received from the client will be office money – see note (xi)(c)(B) below);

(d) as a payment on account of costs generally;

(e) as commission paid in respect of a solicitor's client, unless the client has given the solicitor prior authority to retain it in accordance with rule 2.06 of the Solicitors' Code of Conduct 2007, or unless it falls within the £20 de minimis figure specified in that rule.

(ii) A solicitor to whom a cheque or draft is made out, and who in the course of practice endorses it over to a client or employer, has received client money. Even if no other client money is held or received, the solicitor will be subject to some provisions of the rules, e.g.:

- rule 7 (duty to remedy breaches);

- rule 32 (accounting records for client money);

- rule 34 (production of records);

- rule 35 (delivery of accountants' reports).

(iii) Money held by solicitor liquidators, trustees in bankruptcy, Court of Protection deputies and trustees of occupational pension schemes is client money, subject to a limited application of the rules – see rule 9.

(iv) Money held jointly with another person outside the practice (for example, with a lay trustee, or with another firm of solicitors) is client money subject to a limited application of the rules – see rule 10.

(v) Money held to the sender's order is client money.

(a) If money is accepted on such terms, it must be held in a client account.

(b) However, a cheque or draft sent to a solicitor on terms that the cheque or draft (as opposed to the money) is held to the sender's order must not be presented for payment without the sender's consent.

(c) The recipient is always subject to a professional obligation to return the money, or the cheque or draft, to the sender on demand.

(vi) An advance to a client from the solicitor which is paid into a client account under rule 15(2)(b) becomes client money. For interest, see rule 24(3)(e).

(vii) [deleted]

(viii) If the SRA intervenes in a practice, money from the practice is held or received by the SRA's intervention agent subject to a trust under Schedule 1 paragraph 7(1) of the Solicitors Act 1974, and is therefore client money. The same provision requires the agent to pay the money into a client account.

(ix) A solicitor who, as the donee of a power of attorney, operates the donor's own account is subject to a limited application of these rules – see rule 11. Money kept in the donor's own account is not "client money", because it is not "held or received" by the solicitor.

(x) Money held or received by a solicitor in the course of his or her employment when practising in one of the capacities listed in rule 5 (persons exempt from the rules) is not "client money" for the purpose of the rules, because the rules do not apply at all.

(xi) Office money includes:

(a) money held or received in connection with running the practice; for example, PAYE, or VAT on the firm's fees;

(b) interest on general client accounts; the bank or building society should be instructed to credit such interest to the office account – but see also rule 15(2)(d); and

(c) payments received in respect of:

(A) fees due to the practice against a bill or written notification of costs incurred, which has been given or sent in accordance with rule 19(2);

(B) disbursements already paid by the practice (for definition of "disbursement" see rule 2(2)(k));

(C) disbursements incurred but not yet paid by the practice, but excluding unpaid professional disbursements (for definition of "professional disbursement" see rule 2(2)(s), and note (v) to rule 2);

(D) money paid for or towards an agreed fee – see rule 19(5); and

(d) money held in a client account and earmarked for costs under rule 19(3) (transfer of costs from client account to office account); and

(e) money held or received from the Legal Services Commission as a regular payment (see rule 21(2)).

(xii) A solicitor cannot be his or her own client for the purpose of the rules, so that if a practice conducts a personal or office transaction – for instance, conveyancing – for a principal (or for a number of principals), money held or received on behalf of the principal(s) is office money. However, other circumstances may mean that the money is client money, for example:

(a) If the practice also acts for a lender, money held or received on behalf of the lender is client money.

(b) If the practice acts for a principal and, for example, his or her spouse jointly (assuming the spouse is not a partner in the practice), money received on their joint behalf is client money.

(c) If the practice acts for an assistant solicitor, consultant or non-solicitor employee, or (if it is a company) a director, or (if it is an LLP) a member, he or she is regarded as a client of the practice, and money received for him or her is client money – even if he or she conducts the matter personally.

(xiii) For a flowchart summarising the effect of the rules, see Appendix 1. For more details of the treatment of different types of money, see the chart "Special situations – what applies" at Appendix 2. These two appendices are included to help solicitors and their staff find their way about the rules. Unlike the notes, they are not intended to affect the meaning of the rules.

Part B – Client money and operation of a client account

Rule 14 – Client accounts

(1) A *solicitor* who holds or receives *client money* must keep one or more *client accounts* (unless all the *client money* is always dealt with outside any *client account* in accordance with rule 9, rule 10, rule 16 or rule 17).

(2) A "client account" is an account of a practice kept at a *bank* or *building society* for holding *client money*, in accordance with the requirements of this part of the rules.

(3) The *client account(s)* of:

(a) a sole practitioner must be either in the *solicitor's* own name or in the practice name;

(b) a *partnership* must be in the *firm* name;

(c) an incorporated practice must be in the company name, or the name of the *LLP*;

(d) in-house *solicitors* must be in the name of the current *principal solicitor* or *solicitors*;

(e) *trustees*, where all the *trustees* of a *trust* are *managers* and/or employees of the same *recognised body*, must be either in the name of the *recognised body* or in the name of the *trustee(s)*;

and the name of the account must also include the word "client".

(4) A *client account* must be:

    (a) a *bank* account at a branch (or a *bank's* head office) in England and Wales; or

    (b) a *building society* deposit or share account at a branch (or a society's head office) in England and Wales.

(5) There are two types of *client account*:

    (a) a "separate designated client account", which is a deposit or share account for money relating to a single *client*, other person or *trust*, and which includes in its title, in addition to the requirements of rule 14(3) above, a reference to the identity of the *client*, other person or *trust*; and

    (b) a "general client account", which is any other *client account*.

Notes

(i) For the client accounts of an executor, trustee or nominee company owned by a practice, see rule 31.

(ii) In the case of in-house solicitors, any client account should include the names of all solicitors of the Supreme Court or registered European lawyers held out on the notepaper as principals. The names of other employees who are solicitors of the Supreme Court or registered European lawyers may also be included if so desired. Any person whose name is included will be subject to the full Compensation Fund contribution and his or her name will have to be included on the accountant's report.

(iii) "Bank" and "building society" are defined in rule 2(2)(c) and (d) respectively.

(iv) A practice may have any number of separate designated client accounts and general client accounts.

(v) The word "client" must appear in full; an abbreviation is not acceptable.

(vi) Compliance with rule 14(1) to (4) ensures that clients, as well as the bank or building society, have the protection afforded by section 85 of the Solicitors Act 1974.

(vii) Money held in a client account must be immediately available, even at the sacrifice of interest, unless the client otherwise instructs, or the circumstances clearly indicate otherwise.

Rule 15 – Use of a client account

(1) *Client money* must *without delay* be paid into a *client account*, and must be held in a *client account*, except when the rules provide to the contrary (see rules 9, 10, 16, 17, 19 and 21).

(2) Only *client money* may be paid into or held in a *client account*, except:

(a) an amount of the *solicitor's* own money required to open or maintain the account;

(b) an advance from the *solicitor* to fund a payment on behalf of a *client* or *trust* in excess of funds held for that *client* or *trust*; the sum becomes *client money* on payment into the account (for interest on *client money*, see rule 24(3)(e));

(c) money to replace any sum which for any reason has been drawn from the account in breach of rule 22; the replacement money becomes *client money* on payment into the account; and

(d) a sum in lieu of interest which is paid into a *client account* to enable the *solicitor* to make payment from the *client account* of all money owed to the *client* as an alternative to making separate payments from the *office* and *client accounts*;

and except when the rules provide to the contrary (see note (iv) below).

(3) *Client money* must be returned to the *client* (or other person on whose behalf the money is held) promptly, as soon as there is no longer any proper reason to retain those funds. Payments received after the *solicitor* has already accounted to the *client*, for example by way of a refund, must be paid to the *client* promptly.

(4) A *solicitor* must promptly inform a *client* (or other person on whose behalf the money is held) in writing of the amount of any *client money* retained at the end of a matter (or the substantial conclusion of a matter), and the reason for that retention. The *solicitor* must inform the *client* (or other person) in writing at least once every twelve months thereafter of the amount of *client money* still held and the reason for the retention, for as long as the *solicitor* continues to hold that money.

Notes

(i) See rule 13 and notes for the definition and examples of client money.

(ii) "Without delay" is defined in rule 2(2)(z).

(iii) Exceptions to rule 15(1) (client money must be paid into a client account) can be found in:

- rule 9 – liquidators, trustees in bankruptcy, Court of Protection deputies and trustees of occupational pension schemes;

- rule 10 – joint accounts;

- rule 16 – client's instructions;

- rule 17

    - cash paid straight to client, beneficiary or third party;

    - cheque endorsed to client, beneficiary or third party;

- money withheld from client account on the SRA's authority;

- money withheld from client account in accordance with a trustee's powers;

- rule 19(1)(b) – receipt and transfer of costs;

- rule 21(1) – payments by the Legal Services Commission.

(iv) Rule 15(2)(a) to (d) provides for exceptions to the principle that only client money may be paid into a client account. Additional exceptions can be found in:

- rule 19(1)(c) – receipt and transfer of costs;

- rule 20(2)(b) – receipt of mixed payments;

- rule 21(2)(c)(ii) – transfer to client account of a sum for unpaid professional disbursements, where the solicitor receives regular payments from the Legal Services Commission.

(v) Only a nominal sum will be required to open or maintain an account. In practice, banks will usually open (and, if instructed, keep open) accounts with nil balances.

(vi) [deleted]

(vii) If client money is invested in the purchase of assets other than money – such as stocks or shares – it ceases to be client money, because it is no longer money held by the solicitor. If the investment is subsequently sold, the money received is, again, client money. The records kept under rule 32 must include entries to show the purchase or sale of investments.

(viii) Some schemes proposed by banks would aggregate the sums held in a number of client accounts, including one or more separate designated client accounts, in order to maximise the interest payable. This is acceptable only if:

- each client account remains a separate account;

- the rate of interest applied by the bank is the same for each client account; and

- the bank credits the total amount of the interest earned in respect of each separate designated client account to that account (see rule 24(1)), and credits the interest earned on any general client account to the office account (see note (xi)(b) to rule 13).

(ix) In the case of Wood and Burdett (case number 8669/2002 filed on 13 January 2004), the Solicitors Disciplinary Tribunal said that it is not a proper part of a solicitor's everyday business or practice to operate a banking facility for third parties, whether they are clients of the firm or not. Solicitors should not, therefore, provide banking facilities through a client account. Further, solicitors are likely to lose the exemption under the Financial Services and Markets Act 2000 if a deposit is taken in circumstances which do not form part of a solicitor's practice. It should also be borne in mind that there are criminal sanctions against assisting money launderers.

(x) As with rule 7 (Duty to remedy breaches), "promptly" in rule 15(3) and (4) is not defined but should be given its natural meaning in the particular circumstances. Accounting to a client for any surplus funds will often fall naturally at the end of a matter. Other retainers may be more protracted and, even when the principal work has been completed, funds may still be needed, for example, to cover outstanding work in a conveyancing transaction or to meet a tax liability.

(xi) There may be some instances when, during the course of a retainer, the specific purpose for which particular funds were paid no longer exists, for example, the need to instruct counsel or a medical expert. Rule 15(3) is concerned with returning funds to clients at the end of a matter (or the substantial conclusion of a matter) and is not intended to apply to ongoing retainers. However, solicitors must always act in the best interests of their clients and may need to take instructions in such circumstances to ascertain, for instance, whether the money should be returned to the client or retained to cover the general funding or other aspects of the case.

(xii) (See rule 22(1)(ga)–(h) for withdrawals from a client account when the rightful owner of funds cannot be traced.)

Rule 16 – Client money withheld from client account on client's instructions

(1) *Client money* may be:

    (a) held by the *solicitor* outside a *client account* by, for example, retaining it in the *solicitor's* safe in the form of cash, or placing it in an account in the *solicitor's* name which is not a *client account*, such as an account outside England and Wales; or

    (b) paid into an account at a *bank*, *building society* or other financial institution opened in the name of the *client* or of a person designated by the *client*;

but only if the *client* instructs the *solicitor* to that effect for the *client's* own convenience, and only if the instructions are given in writing, or are given by other means and confirmed by the *solicitor* to the *client* in writing.

(2) It is improper to seek blanket agreements, through standard terms of business or otherwise, to hold *client money* outside a *client account*.

Notes

(i) For advance payments from the Legal Services Commission, withheld from a client account on the Commission's instructions, see rule 21(1)(a).

(ii)   If a client instructs the solicitor to hold part only of a payment in accordance with rule 16(1)(a) or (b), the entire payment must first be placed in a client account. The relevant part can then be transferred out and dealt with in accordance with the client's instructions.

(iii) Money withheld from a client account under rule 16(1)(a) remains client money, and the record-keeping provisions of rule 32, including monthly reconciliations, must be complied with.

(iv)   Once money has been paid into an account set up under rule 16(1)(b), it ceases to be client money. Until that time, the money is client money and a record must therefore be kept of the solicitor's receipt of the money, and its payment into the account in the name of the client or designated person, in accordance with rule 32. If the solicitor can operate the account, the solicitor must comply with rule 11 (operating a client's own account) and rule 33 (accounting records for clients' own accounts). In the absence of instructions to the contrary, any money withdrawn must be paid into a client account – see rule 15(1).

(v)   Clients' instructions under rule 16(1) must be kept for at least six years – see rule 32(9)(d).

(vi)   A payment on account of costs received from a person who is funding all or part of the solicitor's fees may be withheld from a client account on the instructions of that person given in accordance with rule 16(1) and (2).

(vii) For payment of interest, see rule 24(6) and notes (ii) and (iii) to rule 24.

Rule 17 – Other client money withheld from a client account

The following categories of *client money* may be withheld from a *client account*:

(a)   cash received and *without delay* paid in cash in the ordinary course of business to the *client* or, on the *client's* behalf, to a third party, or paid in cash in the execution of a *trust* to a beneficiary or third party;

(b)   a cheque or draft received and endorsed over in the ordinary course of business to the *client* or, on the *client's* behalf, to a third party, or *without delay* endorsed over in the execution of a *trust* to a beneficiary or third party;

(c)   money withheld from a *client account* on instructions under rule 16;

(ca) money which, in accordance with a *trustee's* powers, is paid into or retained in an account of the *trustee* which is not a *client account* (for example, an account outside England and Wales), or properly retained in cash in the performance of the *trustee's* duties;

(d)   unpaid *professional disbursements* included in a payment of *costs* dealt with under rule 19(1)(b);

(e)   (i)   advance payments from the Legal Services Commission withheld from *client account* (see rule 21(1)(a)); and (ii)　unpaid *professional disbursements* included in a payment of *costs* from the Legal Services Commission (see rule 21(1)(b)); and

(f)　money withheld from a *client account* on the written authorisation of the *SRA*. The *SRA* may impose a condition that the *solicitor* pay the money to a charity which gives an indemnity against any legitimate claim subsequently made for the sum received.

Notes

(i)　"Without delay" is defined in rule 2(2)(z).

(ii)　If money is withheld from a client account under rule 17(a) or (b), rule 32 requires records to be kept of the receipt of the money and the payment out.

(iia)　If money is withheld from a client account under rule 17(ca), rule 32 requires a record to be kept of the receipt of the money, and requires the inclusion of the money in the monthly reconciliations.

(iii)　It makes no difference, for the purpose of the rules, whether an endorsement is effected by signature in the normal way or by some other arrangement with the bank.

(iv)　The circumstances in which authorisation would be given under rule 17(f) must be extremely rare. Applications for authorisation should be made to the Professional Ethics Guidance Team.

Rule 18 – [repealed]

Rule 19 – Receipt and transfer of costs

(1)　A *solicitor* who receives money paid in full or part settlement of the *solicitor's* bill (or other notification of *costs*) **must follow one of the following four options:**

    (a)　determine the composition of the payment *without delay*, and deal with the money accordingly:

        (i)　if the sum comprises *office money* only, it must be placed in an *office account*;

        (ii)　if the sum comprises only *client money* (for example an unpaid *professional disbursement* – see rule 2(2)(s), and note (v) to rule 2), the entire sum must be placed in a *client account*;

        (iii)　if the sum includes both *office money* and *client money* (such as unpaid *professional disbursements*; purchase money; or payments in advance for court fees, stamp duty land tax, Land Registry registration fees or telegraphic transfer fees), the *solicitor* must follow rule 20 (receipt of mixed payments); **or**

(b) **ascertain that the payment comprises only *office money,* and/or *client money* in the form of *professional disbursements* incurred but not yet paid, and deal with the payment as follows:**

(i) place the entire sum in an *office account* at a *bank* or *building society* branch (or head office) in England and Wales; and

(ii) by the end of the second working day following receipt, either pay any unpaid *professional disbursement,* or transfer a sum for its settlement to a *client account*; **or**

(c) **pay the entire sum into a *client account* (regardless of its composition), and transfer any *office money* out of the *client account* within 14 days of receipt; or**

(d) **on receipt of *costs* from the Legal Services Commission, follow the option in rule 21(1)(b).**

(2) A *solicitor* who properly requires payment of his or her *fees* from money held for a *client* or *trust* in a *client account* must first give or send a bill of *costs,* or other written notification of the *costs* incurred, to the *client* or the paying party.

(3) Once the *solicitor* has complied with paragraph (2) above, the money earmarked for *costs* becomes *office money* and must be transferred out of the *client account* within 14 days.

(4) A payment on account of *costs* generally is *client money,* and must be held in a *client account* until the *solicitor* has complied with paragraph (2) above. (For an exception in the case of legal aid payments, see rule 21(1)(a).)

(5) A payment for an *agreed fee* must be paid into an *office account.* An "agreed fee" is one that is fixed – not a *fee* that can be varied upwards, nor a *fee* that is dependent on the transaction being completed. An *agreed fee* must be evidenced in writing.

Notes

(i) For the definition and further examples of office and client money, see rule 13 and notes.

(ii) • Money received for paid disbursements is office money.

• Money received for unpaid professional disbursements is client money.

• Money received for other unpaid disbursements for which the solicitor has incurred a liability to the payee (for example, travel agents' charges, taxi fares, courier charges or Land Registry search fees, payable on credit) is office money.

• Money received for disbursements anticipated but not yet incurred is a payment on account, and is therefore client money.

(iii) The option in rule 19(1)(a) allows a solicitor to place all payments in the correct account in the first instance. The option in rule 19(1)(b) allows the prompt banking into an office account of an invoice payment when the only uncertainty is whether or not the payment includes some client money in the form of unpaid professional disbursements. The option in rule 19(1)(c) allows the prompt banking into a client account of any invoice payment in advance of determining whether the payment is a mixture of office and client money (of whatever description) or is only office money.

(iv) A solicitor who is not in a position to comply with the requirements of rule 19(1)(b) cannot take advantage of that option.

(v) The option in rule 19(1)(b) cannot be used if the money received includes a payment on account – for example, a payment for a professional disbursement anticipated but not yet incurred.

(vi) In order to be able to use the option in rule 19(1)(b) for electronic payments or other direct transfers from clients, a solicitor may choose to establish a system whereby clients are given an office account number for payment of costs. The system must be capable of ensuring that, when invoices are sent to the client, no request is made for any client money, with the sole exception of money for professional disbursements already incurred but not yet paid.

(vii) Rule 19(1)(c) allows clients to be given a single account number for making direct payments by electronic or other means – under this option, it has to be a client account.

(viii) A solicitor will not be in breach of rule 19 as a result of a misdirected electronic payment or other direct transfer, provided:

(A) appropriate systems are in place to ensure compliance;

(B) appropriate instructions were given to the client;

(C) the client's mistake is remedied promptly upon discovery; and

(D) appropriate steps are taken to avoid future errors by the client.

(ix) "Properly" in rule 19(2) implies that the work has actually been done, whether at the end of the matter or at an interim stage, and that the solicitor is entitled to appropriate the money for costs.

(x) Costs transferred out of a client account in accordance with rule 19(2) and (3) must be specific sums relating to the bill or other written notification of costs, and covered by the amount held for the particular client or trust. Round sum withdrawals on account of costs will be a breach of the rules.

(xi) In the case of a trust of which the only trustee(s) are within the firm, the paying party will be the trustee(s) themselves. The solicitor must keep the original bill or notification of costs on the file, in addition to complying with rule 32(8) (central record or file of copy bills, etc.).

(xii) Undrawn costs must not remain in a client account as a "cushion" against any future errors which could result in a shortage on that account, and cannot be regarded as available to set off against any general shortage on client account.

(xiii) The rules do not require a bill of costs for an agreed fee, although a solicitor's VAT position may mean that in practice a bill is needed. If there is no bill, the written evidence of the agreement must be filed as a written notification of costs under rule 32(8)(b).

Rule 20 – Receipt of mixed payments

(1) A "mixed payment" is one which includes *client money* as well as *office money*.

(2) A *mixed payment* must either:

   (a) be split between a *client account* and *office account* as appropriate; or

   (b) be placed *without delay* in a *client account*.

(3) If the entire payment is placed in a *client account*, all *office money* must be transferred out of the *client account* within 14 days of receipt.

(4) See rule 19(1)(b) and (c) for additional ways of dealing with (among other things) *mixed payments* received in response to a bill or other notification of *costs*.

(5) See rule 21(1)(b) for (among other things) *mixed payments* received from the Legal Services Commission.

Note

"Without delay" is defined in rule 2(2)(z).

Rule 21 – Treatment of payments to legal aid practitioners

Payments from the Legal Services Commission

(1) Two special dispensations apply to payments (other than *regular payments*) from the Legal Services Commission:

   (a) An advance payment in anticipation of work to be carried out, although *client money*, may be placed in an *office account*, provided the Commission instructs in writing that this may be done.

   (b) A payment for *costs* (interim and/or final) may be paid into an *office account* at a *bank* or *building society* branch (or head office) in England and Wales, regardless of whether it consists wholly of *office money*, or is mixed with *client money* in the form of:

      (i) advance payments for *fees* or *disbursements*; or

(ii)   money for unpaid *professional disbursements*;

provided all money for payment of *disbursements* is transferred to a *client account* (or the *disbursements* paid) within 14 days of receipt.

(2)   The following provisions apply to *regular payments* from the Legal Services Commission:

(a)   "Regular payments" (which are *office money*) are:

(i)   standard monthly payments paid by the Commission under the civil legal aid contracting arrangements;

(ii)   monthly payments paid by the Commission under the criminal legal aid contracting arrangements; and

(iii)   any other payments for work done or to be done received from the Commission under an arrangement for payments on a regular basis.

(b)   *Regular payments* must be paid into an *office account* at a *bank* or *building society* branch (or head office) in England and Wales.

(c)   A *solicitor* must within 28 days of submitting a report to the Commission, notifying completion of a matter, either:

(i)   pay any unpaid *professional disbursement(s)*, or

(ii)   transfer to a *client account* a sum equivalent to the amount of any unpaid *professional disbursement(s)*,

relating to that matter.

(d)   In cases where the Commission permits *solicitors* to submit reports at various stages during a matter rather than only at the end of a matter, the requirement in paragraph (c) above applies to any unpaid *professional disbursement(s)* included in each report so submitted.

Payments from a third party

(3)   If the Legal Services Commission has paid any *costs* to a *solicitor* or a previously nominated *solicitor* in a matter (advice and assistance or legal help *costs*, advance payments or interim *costs*), or has paid *professional disbursements* direct, and *costs* are subsequently settled by a third party:

(a)   The entire third party payment must be paid into a *client account.*

(b)   A sum representing the payments made by the Commission must be retained in the *client account.*

(c)   Any balance belonging to the *solicitor* must be transferred to an *office account* within 14 days of the *solicitor* sending a report to the Commission containing details of the third party payment.

(d)   The sum retained in the *client account* as representing payments made by the Commission must be:

(i)   **either** recorded in the individual *client's* ledger account, and identified as the Commission's money;

(ii)   **or** recorded in a ledger account in the Commission's name, and identified by reference to the *client* or matter;

and kept in the *client account* until notification from the Commission that it has recouped an equivalent sum from subsequent payments due to the *solicitor*. The retained sum must be transferred to an *office account* within 14 days of notification.

Notes

(i)   This rule deals with matters which specifically affect legal aid practitioners. It should not be read in isolation from the remainder of the rules which apply to all solicitors, including legal aid practitioners.

(ii)   Franchised firms can apply for advance payments on the issue of a certificate. The Legal Services Commission has issued instructions that these payments may be placed in office account. For regular payments, see notes (vii)–(x) below.

(iii) Rule 21(1)(b) deals with the specific problems of legal aid practitioners by allowing a mixed or indeterminate payment of costs (or even a payment consisting entirely of unpaid professional disbursements) to be paid into an office account, which for the purpose of rule 21(1)(b) must be an account at a bank or building society. However, it is always open to the solicitor to comply with rule 19(1)(a) to (c), which are the options for all solicitors for the receipt of costs. For regular payments, see notes (vii)–(x) below.

(iv)   Solicitors are required by the Legal Services Commission to report promptly to the Commission on receipt of costs from a third party. It is advisable to keep a copy of the report on the file as proof of compliance with the Commission's requirements, as well as to demonstrate compliance with the rule.

(v)   A third party payment may also include unpaid professional disbursements or outstanding costs of the client's previous solicitor. This part of the payment is client money and must be kept in a client account until the solicitor pays the professional disbursement or outstanding costs.

(vi)   In rule 21, and elsewhere in the rules, references to the Legal Services Commission are to be read, where appropriate, as including the Legal Aid Board.

(vii) Regular payments are office money and are defined as such in the rules (rule 13, note (xi)(e)). They are neither advance payments nor payments of costs for the purposes of the rules. Regular payments must be paid into an office account which for the purpose of rule 21(2)(b) must be an account at a bank or building society.

(viii) Firms in receipt of regular payments must deal with unpaid professional disbursements in the way prescribed by rule 21(2)(c). The rule permits a solicitor who is required to transfer an amount to cover unpaid professional disbursements into a client account to make the transfer from his or her own resources if the regular payments are insufficient.

(ix) The 28 day time limit for paying, or transferring an amount to a client account for, unpaid professional disbursements is for the purposes of these rules only. An earlier deadline may be imposed by contract with the Commission or with counsel, agents or experts. On the other hand, a solicitor may have agreed to pay later than 28 days from the submission of the report notifying completion of a matter, in which case rule 21(2)(c) will require a transfer of the appropriate amount to a client account (but not payment) within 28 days. Solicitors are reminded of their professional obligation to pay the fees of foreign lawyers (see rule 10.07 of the Solicitors' Code of Conduct).

(x)   For the appropriate accounting records for regular payments, see note (v) to rule 32.

Rule 22 – Withdrawals from a client account

(1) *Client money* may only be withdrawn from a *client account* when it is:

(a) properly required for a payment to or on behalf of the *client* (or other person on whose behalf the money is being held);

(aa) properly required for a payment in the execution of a particular *trust*, including the purchase of an investment (other than money) in accordance with the *trustee's* powers;

(b) properly required for payment of a *disbursement* on behalf of the *client* or *trust*;

(c) properly required in full or partial reimbursement of money spent by the *solicitor* on behalf of the *client* or *trust*;

(d) transferred to another *client account*;

(e) withdrawn on the *client's* instructions, provided the instructions are for the *client's* convenience and are given in writing, or are given by other means and confirmed by the *solicitor* to the *client* in writing;

(ea) transferred to an account other than a *client account* (such as an account outside England and Wales), or retained in cash, by a *trustee* in the proper performance of his or her duties;

(f) a refund to the *solicitor* of an advance no longer required to fund a payment on behalf of a *client* or *trust* (see rule 15(2)(b));

(g) money which has been paid into the account in breach of the rules (for example, money paid into the wrong *separate designated client account*) – see paragraph (4) below;

(ga) money not covered by (a) to (g) above, where the *solicitor* complies with the conditions set out in rule 22(2A); or

(h) money not covered by (a) to (g) above, withdrawn from the account on the written authorisation of the *SRA*. The *SRA* may impose a condition that the *solicitor* pay the money to a charity which gives an indemnity against any legitimate claim subsequently made for the sum received.

(2) [deleted]

(2A) A withdrawal of *client money* under paragraph (1)(ga) above may be made only where the amount withdrawn does not exceed £50 in relation to any one individual *client* or *trust* matter and the *solicitor*:

(a) establishes the identity of the owner of the money, or makes reasonable attempts to do so;

(b) makes adequate attempts to ascertain the proper destination of the money, and to return it to the rightful owner, unless the reasonable costs of doing so are likely to be excessive in relation to the amount held;

(c) pays the funds to a charity;

(d) records the steps taken in accordance with paragraphs (a)–(c) above and retains those records, together with all relevant documentation (including receipts from the charity), in accordance with rule 32(8A) and (9)(a); and

(e) keeps a central register in accordance with rule 32(13A).

(3) *Office money* may only be withdrawn from a *client account* when it is:

(a) money properly paid into the account to open or maintain it under rule 15(2)(a);

(b) properly required for payment of the *solicitor's costs* under rule 19(2) and (3);

(c) the whole or part of a payment into a *client account* under rule 19(1)(c);

(d) part of a *mixed payment* placed in a *client account* under rule 20(2)(b); or

(e) money which has been paid into a *client account* in breach of the rules (for example, interest wrongly credited to a *general client account*) – see paragraph (4) below.

(4) Money which has been paid into a *client account* in breach of the rules must be withdrawn from the *client account* promptly upon discovery.

(5) Money withdrawn in relation to a particular *client* or *trust* from a *general client account* must not exceed the money held on behalf of that *client* or *trust* in all the *solicitor's general client accounts* (except as provided in paragraph (6) below).

(6) A *solicitor* may make a payment in respect of a particular *client* or *trust* out of a *general client account*, even if no money (or insufficient money) is held for that *client* or *trust* in the *solicitor's general client account(s)*, provided:

(a) sufficient money is held for that *client* or *trust* in a *separate designated client account*; and

(b) the appropriate transfer from the *separate designated client account* to a *general client account* is made immediately.

(7) Money held for a *client* or *trust* in a *separate designated client account* must not be used for payments for another *client* or *trust*.

(8) A *client account* must not be overdrawn, except in the following circumstances:

(a) A *separate designated client account* of *solicitor-trustee(s)* can be overdrawn if the *trustee(s)* make payments on behalf of the *trust* (for example, inheritance tax) before realising sufficient assets to cover the payments.

(b) If a sole practitioner dies and his or her *client accounts* are frozen, the *solicitor-manager* can operate *client accounts* which are overdrawn to the extent of the money held in the frozen accounts.

Notes

Withdrawals in favour of solicitor, and for payment of disbursements

(i) Disbursements to be paid direct from a client account, or already paid out of the solicitor's own money, can be withdrawn under rule 22(1)(b) or (c) (or rule 22(2)(b) or (c)) in advance of preparing a bill of costs. Money to be withdrawn from a client account for the payment of costs (fees and disbursements) under rule 19(2) and (3) becomes office money and is dealt with under rule 22(3)(b).

(ii) Money is "spent" under rule 22(1)(c) (or rule 22(2)(c)) at the time when the solicitor despatches a cheque, unless the cheque is to be held to the solicitor's order. Money is also regarded as "spent" by the use of a credit account, so that, for example, search fees, taxi fares and courier charges incurred in this way may be transferred to the solicitor's office account.

(iii) See rule 23(3) for the way in which a withdrawal from a client account in favour of the solicitor must be effected.

Cheques payable to banks, building societies, etc.

(iv) In order to protect client money against misappropriation when cheques are made payable to banks, building societies or other large institutions, it is strongly recommended that solicitors add the name and number of the account after the payee's name.

Drawing against uncleared cheques

(v) A solicitor should use discretion in drawing against a cheque received from or on behalf of a client before it has been cleared. If the cheque is not met, other clients' money will have been used to make the payment in breach of the rules. See rule 7 (duty to remedy breaches). A solicitor may be able to avoid a breach of the rules by instructing the bank or building society to charge all unpaid credits to the solicitor's office or personal account.

Non-receipt of telegraphic transfer

(vi)   If a solicitor acting for a client withdraws money from a general client account on the strength of information that a telegraphic transfer is on its way, but the telegraphic transfer does not arrive, the solicitor will have used other clients' money in breach of the rules. See also rule 7 (duty to remedy breaches).

Withdrawals on instructions

(vii) One of the reasons why a client might authorise a withdrawal under rule 22(1)(e) might be to have the money transferred to a type of account other than a client account. If so, the requirements of rule 16 must be complied with.

Withdrawals where the rightful owner cannot be traced, on the SRA's authorisation and without SRA authorisation

(viii) Applications for authorisation under rule 22(1)(h) should be made to the Professional Ethics Guidance Team, who can advise on the criteria which must normally be met for authorisation to be given. Solicitors may under rule 22(1)(ga) pay to a charity sums of £50 or less per client or trust matter without the SRA's authorisation, provided the safeguards set out in rule 22(2A) are followed. Solicitors may, however, if they prefer, apply to the SRA for prior authorisation in all cases.

(viiia) Solicitors will need to apply to the SRA, whatever the amount involved, if the money to be withdrawn is not to be paid to a charity. This situation might arise, for example, if a solicitor has been unable to deliver a bill of costs because the client has become untraceable and so cannot make a transfer from client account to office account in accordance with rule 19(2)–(3).

(ix)   After a practice has been wound up, banks sometimes discover unclaimed balances in an old client account. This money remains subject to rule 22 and rule 23. An application can be made to the SRA under rule 22(1)(h).

(x)   See rule 15(3) and notes (x)–(xi) to rule 15 on the return of client money when there is no longer any reason for its continued retention. See also rule 15(4) on reporting to the client when client money is retained at the end of a matter.

Rule 23 – Method of and authority for withdrawals from client account

(1) A withdrawal from a *client account* may be made only after a specific authority in respect of that withdrawal has been signed by at least one of the following:

   (a) a *solicitor* who holds a current practising certificate or a *registered European lawyer*;

   (b) a Fellow of the Institute of Legal Executives or licensed conveyancer who is a *manager* of the practice, where the practice is a *recognised body*;

   (c) a Fellow of the Institute of Legal Executives or licensed conveyancer who is an employee of the practice, where the practice is a *recognised body* or *recognised sole practitioner*;

   (d) a *registered foreign lawyer* who is a *manager* of the practice, where the practice is a *recognised body*; or

   (e) any other individual who is a *manager* of the practice.

(2) There is no need to comply with paragraph (1) above when transferring money from one *general client account* to another *general client account* at the same *bank* or *building society.*

(3) A withdrawal from a *client account* in favour of the *solicitor* or the practice must be either by way of a cheque to the *solicitor* or practice, or by way of a transfer to the *office account* or to the *solicitor's* personal account. The withdrawal must not be made in cash.

Notes

(a) Reference should also be made to paragraph 4.1.A of the Guidelines for accounting procedures and systems at Appendix 3.

(i) Instructions to the bank or building society to withdraw money from a client account (rule 23(1)) may be given over the telephone, provided a specific authority has been signed in accordance with this rule before the instructions are given. If a solicitor decides to take advantage of this arrangement, it is of paramount importance that the scheme has appropriate in-built safeguards, such as passwords, to give the greatest protection possible for client money. Suitable safeguards will also be needed for practices which operate a CHAPS terminal.

(ii) In the case of a withdrawal by cheque, the specific authority (rule 23(1)) is usually a signature on the cheque itself. Signing a blank cheque is not a specific authority.

(iii) A withdrawal from a client account by way of a private loan from one client to another can only be made if the provisions of rule 30(2) are complied with.

(iv) It is advisable that a withdrawal for payment to or on behalf of a client (or on behalf of a trust) be made by way of a crossed cheque whenever possible.

(v)   Solicitor-trustees who instruct an outside administrator to run, or continue to run, on a day to day basis, the business or property portfolio of an estate or trust will not need to comply with rule 23(1), provided all cheques are retained in accordance with rule 32(10). (See also rule 32, note (ii)(d).)

(vi) Where the sum due to the client is sufficiently large, the solicitor should consider whether it should not appropriately be transferred to the client by direct bank transfer. For doing this, the solicitor would be entitled to make a modest administrative charge in addition to any charge made by the bank in connection with the transfer.

Land Registry application fees paid by direct debit

(vii) Solicitors may set up a direct debit system of payment for Land Registry application fees on either the office account or a client account. If a direct debit payment is to be taken from a client account for the payment of Land Registry application fees, the signature of a person, within one of the categories listed in rule 23(1), on the application for registration will constitute the specific authority required by rule 23(1). As with any other payment method, care must be taken to ensure that sufficient uncommitted funds are held in the client account for the particular client before signing the authority. Solicitors should also bear in mind that should the Land Registry take an incorrect amount in error from a firm's client account (for example, a duplicate payment), the firm will be in breach of the rules if other clients' money has been used as a result.

(viii) If a solicitor fails to specify the correct Land Registry fee on the application for registration (either by specifying a lesser amount than that actually due, or failing to specify any fee at all), the solicitor will be in breach of rule 23(1) if the Land Registry takes a sum from the solicitor's client account greater than that specified on the application, without a specific authority for the revised sum being in place as required by rule 23. In order that the solicitor can comply with the rules, the Land Registry will need to contact the solicitor before taking the revised amount, so that the necessary authority may be signed prior to the revised amount being taken.

(ix) Where the Land Registry contacts the solicitor by telephone, and the solicitor wishes to authorise an immediate payment by direct debit over the telephone, the solicitor will first need to check that there is sufficient money held in client account for the client and, if there is, that it is not committed to some other purpose.

(x)   The specific authority required by rule 23(1) can be signed after the telephone call has ended but must be signed before the additional payment (or correct full payment) is taken by the Land Registry. It is advisable to sign the authority promptly and, in any event, on the same day as the telephone instruction is given to the Land Registry to take the additional (or correct full) amount. If the solicitor decides to fund any extra amount from the office account, the transfer of office money to the client account would need to be made, preferably on the same day but, in any event, before the direct debit is taken. The solicitor's internal procedures would need to make it clear to unqualified staff how to deal with such situations; for example, who they should consult before a direct debit for an amount other than that specified on the application can be authorised, and the mechanism for ensuring the new authority is signed by a person within one of the categories listed in rule 23(1).

(xi)   A solicitor may decide to set up a direct debit system of payment on the office account because, for example, he or she does not wish to allow the Land Registry to have access to the firm's client account. Provided the solicitor is in funds, a transfer from the client account to the office account may be made under rule 22(1)(c) to reimburse the solicitor as soon as the direct debit has been taken.

Part C – Interest

Rule 24 – When interest must be paid

(1)   When a *solicitor* holds money in a *separate designated client account* for a *client*, or for a person funding all or part of the *solicitor's fees*, or for a *trust*, the *solicitor* must account to the *client* or that person or *trust* for all interest earned on the account.

(2)   When a *solicitor* holds money in a *general client account* for a *client*, or for a person funding all or part of the *solicitor's fees*, or for a *trust* (or if money should have been held for a *client* or such other person or *trust* in a *client account* but was not), the *solicitor* must account to the *client* or that person or *trust* for a sum in lieu of interest calculated in accordance with rule 25.

(3)   A *solicitor* is not required to pay a sum in lieu of interest under paragraph (2) above:

(a)   if the amount calculated is £20 or less;

(b)   (i)   if the *solicitor* holds a sum of money not exceeding the amount shown in the left hand column below for a time not exceeding the period indicated in the right hand column:

Amount	Time
£1,000	8 weeks
£2,000	4 weeks
£10,000	2 weeks
£20,000	1 week

(ii)   if the *solicitor* holds a sum of money exceeding £20,000 for one week or less, unless it is fair and reasonable to account for a sum in lieu of interest having regard to all the circumstances;

(c)   on money held for the payment of counsel's fees, once counsel has requested a delay in settlement;

(d)   on money held for the Legal Services Commission;

(e)   on an advance from the *solicitor* under rule 15(2)(b) to fund a payment on behalf of the *client* or *trust* in excess of funds held for that *client* or *trust*; or

(f)   if there is an agreement to contract out of the provisions of this rule under rule 27.

(4)   If sums of money are held intermittently during the course of acting, and the sum in lieu of interest calculated under rule 25 for any period is £20 or less, a sum in lieu of interest should still be paid if it is fair and reasonable in the circumstances to aggregate the sums in respect of the individual periods.

(5)   If money is held for a continuous period, and for part of that period it is held in a *separate designated client account*, the sum in lieu of interest for the rest of the period when the money was held in a *general client account* may as a result be £20 or less. A sum in lieu of interest should, however, be paid if it is fair and reasonable in the circumstances to do so.

(6)   (a)   If a *solicitor* holds money for a *client* (or person funding all or part of the *solicitor's fees*) in an account opened on the instructions of the *client* (or that person) under rule 16(1)(a), the *solicitor* must account to the *client* (or that person) for all interest earned on the account.

     (aa) If a *solicitor-trustee*, whether or not in strict accordance with rule 17(ca), holds money for a *trust* in an account of the *solicitor-trustee* which is not a *client account*, the *solicitor-trustee* must account to the *trust* for all interest earned on the account.

     (b)   If a *solicitor* has failed to comply with instructions to open an account under rule 16(1)(a), the *solicitor* must account to the *client* (or the person funding all or part of the *solicitor's fees*) for a sum in lieu of any net loss of interest suffered by the *client* (or that person) as a result.

(7)   [deleted]

Notes

Requirement to pay interest

(i)   The whole of the interest earned on a separate designated client account must be credited to the account. However, the obligation to pay a sum in lieu of interest for amounts held in a general client account is subject to the de minimis provisions in rule 24(3)(a) and (b). Section 33(3) of the Solicitors Act 1974 permits solicitors to retain any interest earned on client money held in a general client account over and above that which they have to pay under these rules. (See also note (viii) to rule 15 on aggregation of accounts.)

(ii)   There is no requirement to pay a sum in lieu of interest on money held on instructions under rule 16(1)(a) in a manner which attracts no interest.

(iii) Accounts opened in the client's name under rule 16(1)(b) (whether operated by the solicitor or not) are not subject to rule 24, as the money is not held by the solicitor. All interest earned belongs to the client. The same applies to any account in the client's own name operated by the solicitor as signatory under rule 11.

(iv) Money subject to a trust is client money (see rule 13), and rule 24 therefore applies to it.

De minimis provisions (rule 24(3)(a) and (b))

(v) The sum in lieu of interest is calculated over the whole period for which money is held (see rule 25(2)); if this sum is £20 or less, the solicitor need not account to the client, other person or trust. If sums of money are held in relation to separate matters for the same client, other person or trust, it is normally appropriate to treat the money relating to the different matters separately, so that, if any of the sums calculated is £20 or less, no sum in lieu of interest is payable. There will, however, be cases when the matters are so closely related that they ought to be considered together – for example, when a solicitor is acting for a client in connection with numerous debt collection matters.

Administrative charges

(vi) It is not improper to charge a reasonable fee for the handling of client money when the service provided is out of the ordinary.

Unpresented cheques

(vii) A client may fail to present a cheque to his or her bank for payment. Whether or not it is reasonable to recalculate the amount due will depend on all the circumstances of the case. A reasonable charge may be made for any extra work carried out if the solicitor is legally entitled to make such a charge.

Liquidators, trustees in bankruptcy, Court of Protection deputies and trustees of occupational pension schemes

(viii) Under rule 9, Part C of the rules does not normally apply to solicitors who are liquidators, etc. Solicitors must comply with the appropriate statutory rules and regulations, and rules 9(3) and (4) as appropriate.

Joint accounts

(ix) Under rule 10, Part C of the rules does not apply to joint accounts. If a solicitor holds money jointly with a client, interest earned on the account will be for the benefit of the client unless otherwise agreed. If money is held jointly with another solicitors' practice, the allocation of interest earned will depend on the agreement reached.

(x) [deleted]

Failure to pay interest

(xa)   A client, including one of joint clients, or a person funding all or part of a solicitor's fees, may complain to the Legal Complaints Service if he or she believes that interest, or a sum in lieu of interest, was due and has not been paid, or that the amount paid was insufficient. It is advisable for the client (or other person) to try to resolve the matter with the solicitor before approaching the Legal Complaints Service.

Rule 25 – Amount of interest

(1)   *Solicitors* must aim to obtain a reasonable rate of interest on money held in a *separate designated client account*, and must account for a fair sum in lieu of interest on money held in a *general client account* (or on money which should have been held in a *client account* but was not). The sum in lieu of interest need not necessarily reflect the highest rate of interest obtainable but it is not acceptable to look only at the lowest rate of interest obtainable.

(2)   **The sum in lieu of interest** for money held in a *general client account* (or on money which should have been held in a *client account* but was not) **must be calculated**

   •   **on the balance or balances held over the whole period for which cleared funds are held**

   •   **at a rate not less than (whichever is the higher of) the following**

      (i)   the rate of interest payable on a *separate designated client account* for the amount or amounts held, or

      (ii)   the rate of interest payable on the relevant amount or amounts if placed on deposit on similar terms by a member of the business community

   •   **at the *bank* or *building society* where the money is held.**

(3)   If the money, or part of it, is held successively or concurrently in accounts at different *banks* or *building societies*, the relevant *bank* or *building society* for the purpose of paragraph (2) will be whichever of those *banks* or *building societies* offered the best rate on the date when the money was first held.

(4)   If, contrary to the rules, the money held for a *client* or other person is not held in a *client account*, the relevant *bank* or *building society* for the purpose of paragraph (2) will be a clearing *bank* or *building society* nominated by the *client* (or other person).

(5)   If, contrary to the rules, money held by a *solicitor-trustee* is not held in a *client account*, the *solicitor-trustee* has a particular obligation to comply with the requirement in paragraph (1) to account for a fair sum in lieu of interest.

Notes

(i)   The sum in lieu of interest has to be calculated over the whole period for which money is held – see rule 25(2). The solicitor will usually account to the client at the conclusion of the client's matter, but might in some cases consider it appropriate to account to the client at intervals throughout.

(ii)   When looking at the period over which the sum in lieu of interest must be calculated, it will usually be unnecessary to check on actual clearance dates. When money is received by cheque and paid out by cheque, the normal clearance periods will usually cancel each other out, so that it will be satisfactory to look at the period between the dates when the incoming cheque is banked and the outgoing cheque is drawn.

(iii) Different considerations apply when payments in and out are not both made by cheque. So, for example, the relevant periods would normally be:

- from the date when a solicitor receives incoming money in cash until the date when the outgoing cheque is sent;

- from the date when an incoming telegraphic transfer begins to earn interest until the date when the outgoing cheque is sent;

- from the date when an incoming cheque or banker's draft is or would normally be cleared until the date when the outgoing telegraphic transfer is made or banker's draft is obtained.

(iv)   The sum in lieu of interest is calculated by reference to the rates paid by the appropriate bank or building society (see rule 25(2) to (5)). Solicitors will therefore follow the practice of that bank or building society in determining how often interest is compounded over the period for which the cleared funds are held.

(v)   Money held in a client account must be immediately available, even at the sacrifice of interest, unless the client otherwise instructs, or the circumstances clearly indicate otherwise. The need for access can be taken into account in assessing the appropriate rate for calculating the sum to be paid in lieu of interest, or in assessing whether a reasonable rate of interest has been obtained for a separate designated client account.

(vi)   For failure by the solicitor to pay a sufficient sum by way of interest, or in lieu of interest, see note (xa) to rule 24.

Rule 26 – Interest on stakeholder money

When a *solicitor* holds money as stakeholder, the *solicitor* must pay interest, or a sum in lieu of interest, on the basis set out in rule 24 to the person to whom the stake is paid.

Note

For contracting out of this provision, see rule 27(2) and the notes to rule 27.

Rule 27 – Contracting out

(1) In appropriate circumstances a *client* and his or her *solicitor* may by a written agreement come to a different arrangement as to the matters dealt with in rule 24 (payment of interest).

(2) A *solicitor* acting as stakeholder may, by a written agreement with his or her own *client* and the other party to the transaction, come to a different arrangement as to the matters dealt with in rule 24.

Notes

(i)   Solicitors should act fairly towards their clients and provide sufficient information to enable them to give informed consent if it is felt appropriate to depart from the interest provisions. Whether it is appropriate to contract out depends on all the circumstances, for example, the size of the sum involved or the nature, status or bargaining position of the client. It might, for instance, be appropriate to contract out by standard terms of business if the client is a substantial commercial entity and the interest involved is modest in relation to the size of the transaction. The larger the sum of interest involved, the more there would be an onus on the solicitor to show that a client who had accepted a contracting out provision was properly informed and had been treated fairly. Contracting out is never appropriate if it is against the client's interests.

(ii) In principle, a solicitor-stakeholder is entitled to make a reasonable charge to the client for acting as stakeholder in the client's matter.

(iii) Alternatively, it may be appropriate to include a special provision in the contract that the solicitor-stakeholder retains the interest on the deposit to cover his or her charges for acting as stakeholder. This is only acceptable if it will provide a fair and reasonable payment for the work and risk involved in holding a stake. The contract could stipulate a maximum charge, with any interest earned above that figure being paid to the recipient of the stake.

(iv) Any right to charge the client, or to stipulate for a charge which may fall on the client, would be excluded by, for instance, a prior agreement with the client for a fixed fee for the client's matter, or for an estimated fee which cannot be varied upwards in the absence of special circumstances. It is therefore not normal practice for a stakeholder in conveyancing transactions to receive a separate payment for holding the stake.

(v)   A solicitor-stakeholder who seeks an agreement to exclude the operation of rule 26 should be particularly careful not to take unfair advantage either of the client, or of the other party if unrepresented.

Rule 28 – [repealed]

Part D – Accounting systems and records

Rule 29 – Guidelines for accounting procedures and systems

The *SRA* may from time to time publish guidelines for accounting procedures and systems to assist *solicitors* to comply with Parts A to D of the rules, and *solicitors* may be required to justify any departure from the guidelines.

Notes

(i)   The current guidelines appear at Appendix 3.

(ii)   The reporting accountant does not carry out a detailed check for compliance, but has a duty to report on any substantial departures from the guidelines discovered whilst carrying out work in preparation of his or her report (see rules 43 and 44(e)).

Rule 30 – Restrictions on transfers between clients

(1)   A paper transfer of money held in a *general client account* from the ledger of one *client* to the ledger of another *client* may only be made if:

    (a)   it would have been permissible to withdraw that sum from the account under rule 22(1); and

    (b)   it would have been permissible to pay that sum into the account under rule 15;

(but there is no requirement in the case of a paper transfer for the written authority of a *solicitor*, etc., under rule 23(1)).

(2)   No sum in respect of a private loan from one *client* to another can be paid out of funds held for the lender either:

    (a)   by a payment from one *client account* to another;

    (b)   by a paper transfer from the ledger of the lender to that of the borrower; or

    (c)   to the borrower directly,

except with the prior written authority of both *clients*.

Notes

(i)   "Private loan" means a loan other than one provided by an institution which provides loans on standard terms in the normal course of its activities – rule 30(2) does not apply to loans made by an institutional lender. See also the Solicitors' Code of Conduct 2007 rule 3.16(2)(b), which prohibits a solicitor from acting for both lender and borrower in an individual mortgage at arm's length.

(ii)   If the loan is to be made by (or to) joint clients, the consent of each client must be obtained.

Rule 31 – Executor, trustee or nominee companies

(1)   If a *solicitors'* practice owns all the shares in a *recognised body* which is an executor, trustee or nominee company, the practice and the *recognised body* must not operate shared *client accounts*, but may:

    (a)   use one set of accounting records for money held, received or paid by the practice and the *recognised body*; and/or

    (b)   deliver a single accountant's report for both the practice and the *recognised body*.

(2)   If such a *recognised body* as nominee receives a dividend cheque made out to the *recognised body*, and forwards the cheque, either endorsed or subject to equivalent instructions, to the share-owner's *bank* or *building society*, etc., the *recognised body* will have received (and paid) *client money*. One way of complying with rule 32 (accounting records) is to keep a copy of the letter to the share-owner's *bank* or *building society*, etc., on the file, and, in accordance with rule 32(14), to keep another copy in a central book of such letters. (See also rule 32(9)(f) (retention of records for six years).)

Notes [deleted]

Rule 32 – Accounting records for client accounts, etc.

Accounting records which must be kept

(1)   A *solicitor* must at all times keep accounting records properly written up to show the *solicitor's* dealings with:

    (a)   *client money* received, held or paid by the *solicitor*; including *client money* held outside a *client account* under rule 16(1)(a) or rule 17(ca); and

    (b)   [deleted]

    (c)   any *office money* relating to any *client* or *trust* matter.

(2)   All dealings with *client money* must be appropriately recorded:

    (a)   in a client cash account or in a record of sums transferred from one client ledger account to another; and

    (b)   on the client side of a separate client ledger account for each *client* (or other person, or *trust*).

No other entries may be made in these records.

(3)   If *separate designated client accounts* are used:

    (a)   a combined cash account must be kept in order to show the total amount held in *separate designated client accounts*; and

(b) a record of the amount held for each *client* (or other person, or *trust*) must be made either in a deposit column of a client ledger account, or on the client side of a client ledger account kept specifically for a *separate designated client account*, for each *client* (or other person, or *trust*).

(4) All dealings with *office money* relating to any *client* matter, or to any *trust* matter, must be appropriately recorded in an office cash account and on the office side of the appropriate client ledger account.

Current balance

(5) The current balance on each client ledger account must always be shown, or be readily ascertainable, from the records kept in accordance with paragraphs (2) and (3) above.

Acting for both lender and borrower

(6) When acting for both lender and borrower on a mortgage advance, separate client ledger accounts for both *clients* need not be opened, provided that:

(a) the funds belonging to each *client* are clearly identifiable; and

(b) the lender is an institutional lender which provides mortgages on standard terms in the normal course of its activities.

Reconciliations

(7) The *solicitor* must, at least once every fourteen weeks in the case of money held by *solicitor-trustees* in passbook-operated *separate designated client accounts*, and at least once every five weeks in all other cases:

(a) compare the balance on the client cash account(s) with the balances shown on the statements and passbooks (after allowing for all unpresented items) of all *general client accounts* and *separate designated client accounts*, and of any account which is not a *client account* but in which the *solicitor* holds *client money* under rule 16(1)(a) or rule 17(ca), and any *client money* held by the *solicitor* in cash; and

(b) as at the same date prepare a listing of all the balances shown by the client ledger accounts of the liabilities to *clients* (and other persons, and *trusts*) and compare the total of those balances with the balance on the client cash account; and also

(c) prepare a reconciliation statement; this statement must show the cause of the difference, if any, shown by each of the above comparisons.

Bills and notifications of costs

(8)   The *solicitor* must keep readily accessible a central record or file of copies of:

    (a)   all bills given or sent by the *solicitor*; and

    (b)   all other written notifications of *costs* given or sent by the *solicitor*;

    in both cases distinguishing between *fees*, *disbursements* not yet paid at the date of the bill, and paid *disbursements*.

Withdrawals under rule 22(1)(ga)

(8A) A *solicitor* who withdraws *client money* under rule 22(1)(ga) must keep a record of the steps taken in accordance with rule 22(2A)(a)–(c), together with all relevant documentation (including receipts from the charity).

Retention of records

(9)   The *solicitor* must retain for at least six years from the date of the last entry:

    (a)   all documents or other records required by paragraphs (1) to (8A) above;

    (b)   all statements and passbooks, as printed and issued by the *bank, building society* or other financial institution, and/or all duplicate statements and copies of passbook entries permitted in lieu of the originals by rule 10(3) or (4), for:

        (i)   any *general client account* or *separate designated client account*;

        (ii)   any joint account held under rule 10;

        (iii) any account which is not a *client account* but in which the *solicitor* holds *client money* under rule 16(1)(a) or rule 17(ca); and

        (iv) [deleted]

        (v)   any *office account* maintained in relation to the practice;

    (c)   any records kept under rule 9 (liquidators, trustees in bankruptcy, *Court of Protection deputies* and trustees of occupational pension schemes) including, as printed or otherwise issued, any statements, passbooks and other accounting records originating outside the *solicitor's* office;

    (d)   any written instructions to withhold *client money* from a *client account* (or a copy of the *solicitor's* confirmation of oral instructions) in accordance with rule 16;

    (e)   any central registers kept under paragraphs (11) to (13A) below; and

    (f)   any copy letters kept centrally under rule 31(2) (dividend cheques endorsed over by nominee company).

(10) The *solicitor* must retain for at least two years:

    (a) originals or copies of all authorities, other than cheques, for the withdrawal of money from a *client account*; and

    (b) all original paid cheques (or digital images of the front and back of all original paid cheques), unless there is a written arrangement with the *bank, building society* or other financial institution that:

        (i) it will retain the original cheques on the *solicitor's* behalf for that period; or

        (ii) in the event of destruction of any original cheques, it will retain digital images of the front and back of those cheques on the *solicitor's* behalf for that period and will, on demand by the *solicitor*, the *solicitor's* reporting accountant or the *SRA*, produce copies of the digital images accompanied, when requested, by a certificate of verification signed by an authorised officer.

Centrally kept records for certain accounts, etc.

(11) Statements and passbooks for *client money* held outside a *client account* under rule 16(1)(a) or rule 17(ca) must be kept together centrally, or the *solicitor* must maintain a central register of these accounts.

(12) Any records kept under rule 9 (liquidators, trustees in bankruptcy, *Court of Protection deputies* and trustees of occupational pension schemes) must be kept together centrally, or the *solicitor* must maintain a central register of the appointments.

(13) The statements, passbooks, duplicate statements and copies of passbook entries relating to any joint account held under rule 10 must be kept together centrally, or the *solicitor* must maintain a central register of all joint accounts.

(13A) A central register of all withdrawals made under rule 22(1)(ga) must be kept, detailing the name of the *client*, other person or *trust* on whose behalf the money is held (if known), the amount, the name of the recipient charity and the date of the payment.

(14) If a nominee company follows the option in rule 31(2) (keeping instruction letters for dividend payments), a central book must be kept of all instruction letters to the share-owner's *bank* or *building society*, etc.

Computerisation

(15) Records required by this rule may be kept on a computerised system, apart from the following documents, which must be retained as printed or otherwise issued:

    (a) original statements and passbooks retained under paragraph (9)(b) above;

    (b) original statements, passbooks and other accounting records retained under paragraph (9)(c) above; and

(c) original cheques and copy authorities retained under paragraph (10) above.

There is no obligation to keep a hard copy of computerised records. However, if no hard copy is kept, the information recorded must be capable of being reproduced reasonably quickly in printed form for at least six years, or for at least two years in the case of digital images of paid cheques retained under paragraph (10) above.

Suspense ledger accounts

(16) Suspense client ledger accounts may be used only when the *solicitor* can justify their use; for instance, for temporary use on receipt of an unidentified payment, if time is needed to establish the nature of the payment or the identity of the *client*.

Notes

(i) It is strongly recommended that accounting records are written up at least weekly, even in the smallest practice, and daily in the case of larger firms.

(ii) Rule 32(1) to (6) (general record-keeping requirements) and rule 32(7) (reconciliations) do not apply to:

(a) solicitor liquidators, trustees in bankruptcy, Court of Protection deputies and trustees of occupational pension schemes operating in accordance with statutory rules or regulations under rule 9(1)(a);

(b) joint accounts operated under rule 10;

(c) a client's own account operated under rule 11; the record-keeping requirements for this type of account are set out in rule 33;

(d) solicitor-trustees who instruct an outside administrator to run, or continue to run, on a day to day basis, the business or property portfolio of an estate or trust, provided the administrator keeps and retains appropriate accounting records, which are available for inspection by the SRA in accordance with rule 34. (See also note (v) to rule 23.)

(iii) When a cheque or draft is received on behalf of a client and is endorsed over, not passing through a client account, it must be recorded in the books of account as a receipt and payment on behalf of the client. The same applies to cash received and not deposited in a client account but paid out to or on behalf of a client. A cheque made payable to a client, which is forwarded to the client by the solicitor, is not client money and falls outside the rules, although it is advisable to record the action taken.

(iv) For the purpose of rule 32, money which has been paid into a client account under rule 19(1)(c) (receipt of costs), or under rule 20(2)(b) (mixed money), and for the time being remains in a client account, is to be treated as client money; it should be recorded on the client side of the client ledger account, but must be appropriately identified.

(v)   For the purpose of rule 32, money which has been paid into an office account under rule 19(1)(b) (receipt of costs), rule 21(1)(a) (advance payments from the Legal Services Commission), or under rule 21(1)(b) (payment of costs from the Legal Services Commission), and for the time being remains in an office account without breaching the rules, is to be treated as office money. Money paid into an office account under rule 21(2)(b) (regular payments) is office money. All these payments should be recorded on the office side of the client ledger account (for the individual client or for the Legal Services Commission), and must be appropriately identified.

(vi)   Some accounting systems do not retain a record of past daily balances. This does not put the solicitor in breach of rule 32(5).

(vii) "Clearly identifiable" in rule 32(6) means that by looking at the ledger account the nature and owner of the mortgage advance are unambiguously stated. For example, if a mortgage advance of £100,000 is received from the ABC Building Society, the entry should be recorded as "£100,000, mortgage advance, ABC Building Society". It is not enough to state that the money was received from the ABC Building Society without specifying the nature of the payment, or vice versa.

(viii) Although the solicitor does not open a separate ledger account for the lender, the mortgage advance credited to that account belongs to the lender, not to the borrower, until completion takes place. Improper removal of these mortgage funds from a client account would be a breach of rule 22.

(ix)   Reconciliations should be carried out as they fall due, and in any event no later than the due date for the next reconciliation. In the case of a separate designated client account operated with a passbook, there is no need to ask the bank, building society or other financial institution for confirmation of the balance held. In the case of other separate designated client accounts, the solicitor should either obtain statements at least monthly, or should obtain written confirmation of the balance direct from the bank, building society or other financial institution. There is no requirement to check that interest has been credited since the last statement, or the last entry in the passbook.

(x)   In making the comparisons under rule 32(7)(a) and (b), some solicitors use credits of one client against debits of another when checking total client liabilities. This is improper because it fails to show up the shortage.

(xi)   The effect of rule 32(9)(b) is that the solicitor must ensure that the bank issues hard copy statements. Statements sent from the bank to its solicitor customer by means of electronic mail, even if capable of being printed off as hard copies, will not suffice.

(xii) Rule 32(9)(d) – retention of client's instructions to withhold money from a client account – does not require records to be kept centrally; however this may be prudent, to avoid losing the instructions if the file is passed to the client.

(xiii) A solicitor who holds client money in a currency other than sterling should hold that money in a separate account for the appropriate currency. Separate books of account should be kept for that currency.

(xiv) The requirement to keep paid cheques under rule 32(10)(b) extends to all cheques drawn on a client account, or on an account in which client money is held outside a client account under rule 16(1)(a) or rule 17(ca).

(xv) Solicitors may enter into an arrangement whereby the bank keeps digital images of paid cheques in place of the originals. The bank should take an electronic image of the front and back of each cheque in black and white and agree to hold such images, and to make printed copies available on request, for at least two years. Alternatively, solicitors may take and keep their own digital images of paid cheques.

(xvi) Microfilmed copies of paid cheques are not acceptable for the purposes of rule 32(10)(b). If a bank is able to provide microfilmed copies only, the solicitor must obtain the original paid cheques from the bank and retain them for at least two years.

(xvii) Certificates of verification in relation to digital images of cheques may on occasion be required by the SRA when exercising its investigative and enforcement powers. The reporting accountant will not need to ask for a certificate of verification but will be able to rely on the printed copy of the digital image as if it were the original.

Rule 33 – Accounting records for clients' own accounts

(1) When a *solicitor* operates a *client's* own account as signatory under rule 11, the *solicitor* must retain, for at least six years from the date of the last entry, the statements or passbooks as printed and issued by the *bank*, *building society* or other financial institution, and/or the duplicate statements, copies of passbook entries and cheque details permitted in lieu of the originals by rule 11(3) or (4); and any central register kept under paragraph (2) below.

(2) The *solicitor* must either keep these records together centrally, or maintain a central register of the accounts operated under rule 11.

(3) If, when the *solicitor* ceases to operate the account, the *client* requests the original statements or passbooks, the *solicitor* must take photocopies and keep them in lieu of the originals.

(4) This rule applies only to *solicitors* in private practice.

Note

Solicitors should remember the requirements of rule 32(8) (central record of bills, etc.).

Part E – Monitoring and investigation by the SRA

Rule 34 – Production of records

(1) Any *solicitor* must at the time and place fixed by the *SRA* produce to any person appointed by the *SRA* any records, papers, *client* and *trust* matter files, financial accounts and other documents, and any other information, necessary to enable preparation of a report on compliance with the rules.

(2) A requirement for production under paragraph (1) above must be in writing, and left at or sent by the "recorded signed for" or "special delivery next day" service to the most recent address held by the *SRA's* Information Directorate, or delivered by the *SRA's* appointee. If sent through the post, receipt will be deemed 48 hours (excluding Saturdays, Sundays and Bank Holidays) after posting.

(3) Material kept electronically must be produced in the form required by the *SRA's* appointee.

(4) The *SRA's* appointee is entitled to seek verification from *clients* and staff, and from the *banks*, *building societies* and other financial institutions used by the *solicitor*. The *solicitor* must, if necessary, provide written permission for the information to be given.

(5) The *SRA's* appointee is not entitled to take original documents away but must be provided with photocopies on request.

(6) A *solicitor* must be prepared to explain and justify any departures from the guidelines for accounting procedures and systems published by the *SRA* (see rule 29).

(7) Any report made by the *SRA's* appointee may, if appropriate, be sent to the Crown Prosecution Service or the Serious Fraud Office and/or used in proceedings before the Solicitors Disciplinary Tribunal. In the case of a *registered European lawyer* or *registered foreign lawyer*, the report may also be sent to the competent authority in that lawyer's home state or states. In the case of a *solicitor of the Supreme Court* who is established in another state under the Establishment of Lawyers Directive 98/5/EC, the report may also be sent to the competent authority in the host state. The report may also be sent to any of the accountancy bodies set out in rule 37(1)(a) and/or taken into account by the *SRA* in relation to a possible disqualification of a reporting accountant under rule 37(3).

(8) Without prejudice to paragraph (1) above, any *solicitor* must produce documents relating to any account kept by the *solicitor* at a *bank* or with a *building society*:

    (a) in connection with the *solicitor's* practice; or

    (b) in connection with any *trust* of which the *solicitor* is or formerly was a *trustee*,

for inspection by a person appointed by the *SRA* for the purpose of preparing a report on compliance with the rules or on whether the account has been used for or in connection with a breach of any other rules, codes or mandatory guidance made or issued by the *SRA*. Paragraphs (2)–(7) above apply in relation to this paragraph in the same way as to paragraph (1).

Notes

(i)   "Solicitor" in rule 34 (as elsewhere in the rules) includes any person to whom the rules apply – see rule 2(2)(x), rule 4 and note (ii) to rule 4.

(ii)   The SRA's powers override any confidence or privilege between solicitor and client.

(iii) The SRA's monitoring and investigation powers are exercised by Forensic Investigations.

(iv)   Reasons are never given for a visit by Forensic Investigations, so as:

   (a) to safeguard the SRA's sources of information; and

   (b) not to alert a defaulting manager or employee to conceal or compound his or her misappropriations.

(v)   [deleted]

Part F – Accountants' reports

Rule 35 – Delivery of accountants' reports

(1) A *solicitor* who or which has, at any time during an *accounting period*, held or received *client money*, or operated a *client's* own account as signatory, must deliver to the *SRA* an accountant's report for that *accounting period* within six months of the end of the *accounting period*. This duty extends to the directors of a company, or the members of an *LLP*, which is subject to this rule.

(2) In addition the *SRA* may require the delivery of an accountant's report in circumstances other than those set out in paragraph (1) above if the *SRA* has reason to believe that it is in the public interest to do so.

Notes

(i)   Examples of situations under rule 35(2) include:

   • when no report has been delivered but the SRA has reason to believe that a report should have been delivered;

   • when a report has been delivered but the SRA has reason to believe that it may be inaccurate;

   • when the conduct of the solicitor gives the SRA reason to believe that it would be appropriate to require earlier delivery of a report (for instance three months after the end of the accounting period);

- when the conduct of the solicitor gives the SRA reason to believe that it would be appropriate to require more frequent delivery of reports (for instance every six months);

- when the SRA has reason to believe that the regulatory risk justifies the imposition on a category of solicitors of a requirement to deliver reports earlier or at more frequent intervals;

- when a condition on a solicitor's practising certificate requires earlier delivery of reports or the delivery of reports at more frequent intervals.

(ii) For accountant's reports of limited scope see rule 9 (liquidators, trustees in bankruptcy, Court of Protection deputies and trustees of occupational pension schemes), rule 10 (joint accounts) and rule 11 (operation of a client's own account). For exemption from the obligation to deliver a report, see rule 5 (persons exempt from the rules).

(iii) The requirement in rule 35 for a registered foreign lawyer to deliver an accountant's report applies only to a registered foreign lawyer practising in one of the ways set out in rule 2(2)(x)(iii).

(iv) The form of report is dealt with in rule 47.

(v) When client money is held or received by an unincorporated practice, the principals in the practice will have held or received client money. A salaried partner whose name appears in the list of partners on a firm's letterhead, even if the name appears under a separate heading of "salaried partners" or "associate partners", is a principal.

(va) In the case of an incorporated practice, it is the company or LLP (i.e. the recognised body) which will have held or received client money. The recognised body and its directors (in the case of a company) or members (in the case of an LLP) will have the duty to deliver an accountant's report, although the directors or members will not usually have held client money

(vi) Assistant solicitors, consultants and other employees do not normally hold client money. An assistant solicitor or consultant might be a signatory for a firm's client account, but this does not constitute holding or receiving client money. If a client or third party hands cash to an assistant solicitor, consultant or other employee, it is the sole principal or the partners (rather than the assistant solicitor, consultant or other employee) who are regarded as having received and held the money. In the case of an incorporated practice, whether a company or an LLP, it would be the recognised body itself which would be regarded as having held or received the money.

(vii) If, exceptionally, an assistant solicitor, consultant or other employee has a client account (as a trustee), or operates a client's own account as signatory, the assistant solicitor, consultant or other employee will have to deliver an accountant's report. The assistant solicitor, consultant or other employee can be included in the report of the practice, but must ensure that his or her name is added, and an explanation given.

(viii) A solicitor to whom a cheque or draft is made out, and who in the course of practice endorses it over to a client or employer, has received (and paid) client money. That solicitor will have to deliver an accountant's report, even if no other client money has been held or received.

(ix) When only a small number of transactions is undertaken or a small volume of client money is handled in an accounting period, a waiver of the obligation to deliver a report may sometimes be granted. Applications should be made to the Information Directorate.

(x) If a solicitors' practice owns all the shares in a recognised body which is an executor, trustee or nominee company, the practice and the recognised body may deliver a single accountant's report (see rule 31(1)(b)).

Rule 36 – Accounting periods

The norm

(1) An "accounting period" means the period for which the accounts of the *solicitor* are ordinarily made up, except that it must:

(a) begin at the end of the previous *accounting period*; and

(b) cover twelve months.

Paragraphs (2) to (5) below set out exceptions.

First and resumed reports

(2) For a *solicitor* who is under a duty to deliver his or her first report, the *accounting period* must begin on the date when the *solicitor* first held or received *client money* (or operated a *client's* own account as signatory), and may cover less than twelve months.

(3) For a *solicitor* who is under a duty to deliver his or her first report after a break, the *accounting period* must begin on the date when the *solicitor* for the first time after the break held or received *client money* (or operated a *client's* own account as signatory), and may cover less than twelve months.

Change of accounting period

(4) If a practice changes the period for which its accounts are made up (for example, on a merger, or simply for convenience), the *accounting period* immediately preceding the change may be shorter than twelve months, or longer than twelve months up to a maximum of 18 months, provided that the *accounting period* shall not be changed to a period longer than twelve months unless the *SRA* receives written notice of the change before expiry of the deadline for

delivery of the accountant's report which would have been expected on the basis of the *firm's* old *accounting period.*

Final reports

(5) A *solicitor* who for any reason stops holding or receiving *client money* (and operating any *client's* own account as signatory) must deliver a final report. The *accounting period* must end on the date upon which the *solicitor* stopped holding or receiving *client money* (and operating any *client's* own account as signatory), and may cover less than twelve months.

Notes

(i)   In the case of solicitors joining or leaving a continuing partnership, any accountant's report for the practice as a whole will show the names and dates of the principals joining or leaving. For a solicitor who did not previously hold or receive client money, etc., and has become a principal in the firm, the report for the practice will represent, from the date of joining, the solicitor's first report for the purpose of rule 36(2). For a solicitor who was a principal in the firm and, on leaving, stops holding or receiving client money, etc., the report for the practice will represent, up to the date of leaving, the solicitor's final report for the purpose of rule 36(5) above.

(ii) When a partnership splits up, it is usually appropriate for the books to be made up as at the date of dissolution, and for an accountant's report to be delivered within six months of that date. If, however, the old partnership continues to hold or receive client money, etc., in connection with outstanding matters, accountant's reports will continue to be required for those matters; the books should then be made up on completion of the last of those matters and a report delivered within six months of that date. The same would be true for a sole practitioner winding up matters on retirement.

(iii) When a practice is being wound up, the solicitor may be left with money which is unattributable, or belongs to a client who cannot be traced. It may be appropriate to apply to the SRA for authority to withdraw this money from the solicitor's client account – see rule 22(1)(h), and note (viii) to rule 22.

Rule 37 – Qualifications for making a report

(1)   A report must be prepared and signed by an accountant

    (a)   who is a member of:

        (i)   the Institute of Chartered Accountants in England and Wales;

        (ii)   the Institute of Chartered Accountants of Scotland;

        (iii) the Association of Chartered Certified Accountants;

(iv)   the Institute of Chartered Accountants in Ireland; or

(v)   the Association of Authorised Public Accountants; **and**

(b) who is also:

(i)   an individual who is a registered auditor within the terms of section 35(1)(a) of the Companies Act 1989; or

(ii)   an employee of such an individual; or

(iii) a *partner* in or employee of a *partnership* which is a registered auditor within the terms of section 35(1)(a) of the Companies Act 1989; or

(iv)   a director or employee of a company which is a registered auditor within the terms of section 35(1)(a) of the Companies Act 1989; or

(v)   a member or employee of an *LLP* which is a registered auditor within the terms of section 35(1)(a) of the Companies Act 1989.

(2) An accountant is not qualified to make a report if:

(a)   at any time between the beginning of the *accounting period* to which the report relates, and the completion of the report:

(i)   he or she was a *partner* or employee, or an officer or employee (in the case of a company), or a member or employee (in the case of an *LLP*) in the practice to which the report relates; or

(ii)   he or she was employed by the same *non-solicitor employer* as the *solicitor* for whom the report is being made; or

(b)   he or she has been disqualified under paragraph (3) below and notice of disqualification has been given under paragraph (4) (and has not subsequently been withdrawn).

(3) The *SRA* may disqualify an accountant from making any accountant's report if:

(a)   the accountant has been found guilty by his or her professional body of professional misconduct or discreditable conduct; or

(b)   the *SRA* is satisfied that a *solicitor* has not complied with the rules in respect of matters which the accountant has negligently failed to specify in a report.

In coming to a decision, the *SRA* will take into account any representations made by the accountant or his or her professional body.

(4) Written notice of disqualification must be left at or sent by recorded delivery to the address of the accountant shown on an accountant's report or in the records of the accountant's professional body. If sent through the post, receipt will be deemed 48 hours (excluding Saturdays, Sundays and Bank Holidays) after posting.

(5) An accountant's disqualification may be notified to any *solicitor* likely to be affected and may be printed in the Law Society's Gazette or other publication.

Note

It is not a breach of the rules for a solicitor to retain an outside accountant to write up the books of account and to instruct the same accountant to prepare the accountant's report. However, the accountant will have to disclose these circumstances in the report – see the form of report in Appendix 5.

Rule 38 – Reporting accountant's rights and duties – letter of engagement

(1) The *solicitor* must ensure that the reporting accountant's rights and duties are stated in a letter of engagement incorporating the following terms:

"In accordance with rule 38 of the Solicitors' Accounts Rules 1998, you are instructed as follows:

(i) I/this firm/this company/this limited liability partnership recognises that, if during the course of preparing an accountant's report:

(a) you discover evidence of fraud or theft in relation to money

- held by a solicitor (or registered European lawyer, or registered foreign lawyer, or recognised body, or employee of a solicitor or registered European lawyer, or manager or employee of a recognised body) for a client or any other person (including money held on trust), or

- held in an account of a client, or an account of another person, which is operated by a solicitor (or registered European lawyer, registered foreign lawyer, recognised body, employee of a solicitor or registered European lawyer, or manager or employee of a recognised body); or

(b) you obtain information which you have reasonable cause to believe is likely to be of material significance in determining whether a solicitor (or registered European lawyer, or registered foreign lawyer, or recognised body, or employee of a solicitor or registered European lawyer, or manager or employee of a recognised body) is a fit and proper person

- to hold money for clients or other persons (including money held on trust), or

- to operate an account of a client or an account of another person,

you must immediately give a report of the matter to the Solicitors Regulation Authority in accordance with section 34(9) of the Solicitors Act 1974;

(ii) you may, and are encouraged to, make that report without prior reference to me/this firm/this company/this limited liability partnership;

(iii) you are to report directly to the Solicitors Regulation Authority should your appointment be terminated following the issue of, or indication of intention to issue, a qualified accountant's report, or following the raising of concerns prior to the preparation of an accountant's report;

(iv) you are to deliver to me/this firm/this company/this limited liability partnership with your report the completed checklist required by rule 46 of the Solicitors' Accounts Rules 1998; to retain for at least three years from the date of signature a copy of the completed checklist; and to produce the copy to the Solicitors Regulation Authority on request;

(v) you are to retain these terms of engagement for at least three years after the termination of the retainer and to produce them to the Solicitors Regulation Authority on request; and

(vi) following any direct report made to the Solicitors Regulation Authority under (i) or (iii) above, you are to provide to the Solicitors Regulation Authority on request any further relevant information in your possession or in the possession of your firm.

To the extent necessary to enable you to comply with (i) to (vi) above, I/we waive my/the firm's/the company's/the limited liability partnership's right of confidentiality. This waiver extends to any report made, document produced or information disclosed to the Solicitors Regulation Authority in good faith pursuant to these instructions, even though it may subsequently transpire that you were mistaken in your belief that there was cause for concern."

(2) The letter of engagement and a copy must be signed by the *solicitor* (or by a *partner*, or in the case of a company by a director, or in the case of an *LLP* by a member) and by the accountant. The *solicitor* must keep the copy of the signed letter of engagement for at least three years after the termination of the retainer and produce it to the *SRA* on request.

Notes

(i)   Any direct report by the accountant to the SRA under rule 38(1)(i) or (iii) should be made to the Fraud and Confidential Intelligence Bureau.

(ii)   Rule 38(1) envisages that the specified terms are incorporated in a letter from the solicitor to the accountant. Instead, the specified terms may be included in a letter from the accountant to the solicitor setting out the terms of the engagement. If so, the text must be adapted appropriately. The letter must be signed in duplicate by both parties – the solicitor will keep the original, and the accountant the copy.

Rule 39 – Change of accountant

On instructing an accountancy practice to replace that previously instructed to produce accountant's reports, the *solicitor* must immediately notify the *SRA* of the change and provide the name and business address of the new accountancy practice.

Rule 40 – Place of examination

Unless there are exceptional circumstances, the place of examination of a *solicitor's* accounting records, files and other relevant documents must be the *solicitor's* office and not the office of the accountant. This does not prevent an initial electronic transmission of data to the accountant for examination at the accountant's office with a view to reducing the time which needs to be spent at the *solicitor's* office.

Rule 41 – Provision of details of bank accounts, etc.

The accountant must request, and the *solicitor* must provide, details of all accounts kept or operated by the *solicitor* in connection with the *solicitor's* practice at any *bank*, *building society* or other financial institution at any time during the *accounting period* to which the report relates. This includes *client accounts*, *office accounts*, accounts which are not *client accounts* but which contain *client money*, and *clients'* own accounts operated by the *solicitor* as signatory.

Rule 42 – Test procedures

(1) The accountant must examine the accounting records (including statements and passbooks), *client* and *trust* matter files selected by the accountant as and when appropriate, and other relevant documents of the *solicitor*, and make the following checks and tests:

    (a) confirm that the accounting system in every office of the *solicitor* complies with:

       • rule 32 – accounting records for *client accounts*, etc;

       • rule 33 – accounting records for clients' own accounts;

    and is so designed that:

       (i) an appropriate client ledger account is kept for each *client* (or other person for whom *client money* is received, held or paid) or *trust*;

       (ii) the client ledger accounts show separately from other information details of all *client money* received, held or paid on account of each *client* (or other person for whom *client money* is received, held or paid) or *trust*; and

       (iii) transactions relating to *client money* and any other money dealt with through a *client account* are recorded in the accounting records in a way which distinguishes them from transactions relating to any other money received, held or paid by the *solicitor*;

(b) make test checks of postings to the client ledger accounts from records of receipts and payments of *client money*, and make test checks of the casts of these accounts and records;

(c) compare a sample of payments into and from the *client accounts* as shown in *bank* and *building society* statements or passbooks with the *solicitor's* records of receipts and payments of *client money*;

(d) test check the system of recording *costs* and of making transfers in respect of *costs* from the *client accounts*;

(e) make a test examination of a selection of documents requested from the *solicitor* in order to confirm:

　(i) that the financial transactions (including those giving rise to transfers from one client ledger account to another) evidenced by such documents comply with Parts A and B of the rules, rule 30 (restrictions on transfers between clients) and rule 31 (executor, trustee or nominee companies); and

　(ii) that the entries in the accounting records reflect those transactions in a manner complying with rule 32;

(f) subject to paragraph (2) below, extract (or check extractions of) balances on the client ledger accounts during the *accounting period* under review at not fewer than two dates selected by the accountant (one of which may be the last day of the *accounting period*), and at each date:

　(i) compare the total shown by the client ledger accounts of the liabilities to the *clients* (and other persons for whom *client money* is held) and *trusts* with the cash account balance; and

　(ii) reconcile that cash account balance with the balances held in the *client accounts*, and accounts which are not *client accounts* but in which *client money* is held, as confirmed direct to the accountant by the relevant *banks*, *building societies* and other financial institutions;

(g) confirm that reconciliation statements have been made and kept in accordance with rule 32(7) and (9)(a);

(h) make a test examination of the client ledger accounts to see whether payments from the *client account* have been made on any individual account in excess of money held on behalf of that *client* (or other person for whom *client money* is held) or *trust*;

(i) check the office ledgers, office cash accounts and the statements provided by the *bank*, *building society* or other financial institution for any *office account* maintained by the *solicitor* in connection with the practice, to see whether any *client money* has been improperly paid into an *office account* or, if properly paid into an *office account* under rule 19(1)(b) or rule 21(1), has been kept there in breach of the rules;

(j) check the accounting records kept under rule 32(9)(d) and (11) for *client money* held outside a *client account* to ascertain what transactions have been effected in respect of this money and to confirm that the *client* has given appropriate instructions under rule 16(1)(a);

(k) make a test examination of the client ledger accounts to see whether rule 32(6) (accounting records when acting for both lender and borrower) has been complied with;

(l) for liquidators, trustees in bankruptcy, *Court of Protection deputies* and trustees of occupational pension schemes, check that records are being kept in accordance with rule 32(8), (9)(c) and (12), and cross-check transactions with *client* or *trust* matter files when appropriate;

(m) check that statements and passbooks and/or duplicate statements and copies of passbook entries are being kept in accordance with rule 32(9)(b) (ii) and (13) (record-keeping requirements for joint accounts), and cross-check transactions with *client* matter files when appropriate;

(n) check that statements and passbooks and/or duplicate statements, copies of passbook entries and cheque details are being kept in accordance with rule 33 (record-keeping requirements for clients' own accounts), and cross-check transactions with *client* matter files when appropriate;

(na) for money withdrawn from *client account* under rule 22(1)(ga), check that records are being kept in accordance with rule 32(8A), (9)(a) and (13A), and cross-check with *client* or *trust* matter files when appropriate;

(o) check that interest earned on *separate designated client accounts*, and in accounts opened on *clients'* instructions under rule 16(1)(a), is credited in accordance with rule 24(1) and (6)(a), and note (i) to rule 24;

(p) in the case of private practice only, check that for the period which will be covered by the accountant's report the practice was covered for the purposes of the Solicitors' Indemnity Insurance Rules in respect of its offices in England and Wales by:

- certificates of qualifying insurance outside the assigned risks pool; or

- a policy issued by the assigned risks pool manager; or

- certificates of indemnity cover under the professional requirements of a *registered European lawyer's* home jurisdiction in accordance with paragraph 1 of Appendix 3 to those Rules, together with the *SRA's* written grant of full exemption; or

- certificates of indemnity cover under the professional requirements of a *registered European lawyer's* home jurisdiction plus certificates of a difference in conditions policy with a qualifying insurer under paragraph 2 of Appendix 3 to those Rules, together with the *SRA's* written grant of partial exemption; and

(q) ask for any information and explanations required as a result of making the above checks and tests.

Extracting balances

(2) For the purposes of paragraph (1)(f) above, if a *solicitor* uses a computerised or mechanised system of accounting which automatically produces an extraction

of all client ledger balances, the accountant need not check all client ledger balances extracted on the list produced by the computer or machine against the individual records of client ledger accounts, provided the accountant:

(a) confirms that a satisfactory system of control is in operation and the accounting records are in balance;

(b) carries out a test check of the extraction against the individual records; and

(c) states in the report that he or she has relied on this exception.

Notes

(i) The rules do not require a complete audit of the solicitor's accounts nor do they require the preparation of a profit and loss account or balance sheet.

(ii) In making the comparisons under rule 42(1)(f), some accountants improperly use credits of one client against debits of another when checking total client liabilities, thus failing to disclose a shortage. A debit balance on a client account when no funds are held for that client results in a shortage which must be disclosed as a result of the comparison.

(iii) The main purpose of confirming balances direct with banks, etc., under rule 42(1)(f)(ii) is to ensure that the solicitor's records accurately reflect the sums held at the bank. The accountant is not expected to conduct an active search for undisclosed accounts.

(iv) In checking compliance with rule 22(1)(ga), the accountant should check on a sample basis that the solicitor has complied with rule 22(2A) and is keeping appropriate records in accordance with rules 32(8A), (9)(a) and (13A). The accountant is not expected to judge the adequacy of the steps taken to establish the identity of, and to trace, the rightful owner of the money.

Rule 43 – Departures from guidelines for accounting procedures and systems

The accountant should be aware of the *SRA's* guidelines for accounting procedures and systems (see rule 29), and must note in the accountant's report any substantial departures from the guidelines discovered whilst carrying out work in preparation of the report. (See also rule 44(e).)

Rule 44 – Matters outside the accountant's remit

The accountant is not required:

(a) to extend his or her enquiries beyond the information contained in the documents produced, supplemented by any information and explanations given by the *solicitor*;

(b)   to enquire into the stocks, shares, other securities or documents of title held by the *solicitor* on behalf of the *solicitor's clients*;

(c)   to consider whether the accounting records of the *solicitor* have been properly written up at any time other than the time at which his or her examination of the accounting records takes place;

(d)   to check compliance with the provisions in rule 24(2) to (5) and (6)(b) on payment of sums in lieu of interest;

(e)   to make a detailed check on compliance with the guidelines for accounting procedures and systems (see rules 29 and 43); or

(f)   to determine the adequacy of the steps taken under paragraphs (a) and (b) of rule 22(2A).

Rule 45 – Privileged documents

A *solicitor*, acting on a *client's* instructions, will normally have the right on the grounds of privilege as between *solicitor* and *client* to decline to produce any document requested by the accountant for the purposes of his or her examination. In these circumstances, the accountant must qualify the report and set out the circumstances.

Note

In a recognised body with one or more managers who are not legally qualified, legal professional privilege may not attach to work which is neither done nor supervised by a legally qualified individual – see Legal Services Act 2007, section 190(3) to (7), and Schedule 22, paragraph 17.

Rule 46 – Completion of checklist

The accountant should exercise his or her professional judgment in adopting a suitable "audit" programme, but must also complete and sign a checklist in the form published from time to time by the *SRA*. The *solicitor* must obtain the completed checklist, retain it for at least three years from the date of signature and produce it to the *SRA* on request.

Notes

(i)   The current checklist appears at Appendix 4. It is issued by the SRA to solicitors at the appropriate time for completion by their reporting accountants.

(ii)   The letter of engagement required by rule 38 imposes a duty on the accountant to hand the completed checklist to the solicitor, to keep a copy for three years and to produce the copy to the SRA on request.

Rule 47 – Form of accountant's report

The accountant must complete and sign his or her report in the form published from time to time by the *SRA*.

Notes

(i)   The current form of accountant's report appears at Appendix 5.

(ii)   The form of report is prepared and issued by the SRA to solicitors at the appropriate time for completion by their reporting accountants. Separate reports can be delivered for each principal in a partnership but most firms deliver one report in the name of all the principals. For assistant solicitors, consultants and other employees, see rule 35, notes (vi) and (vii).

(iia)   An incorporated practice will deliver only one report, on behalf of the company and its directors, or on behalf of the LLP and its members – see rule 35(1).

(iii)   Although it may be agreed that the accountant send the report direct to the SRA, the responsibility for delivery is that of the solicitor. The form of report requires the accountant to confirm that either a copy of the report has been sent to each of the persons (including bodies corporate) to whom the report relates, or a copy of the report has been sent to a named partner on behalf of all the partners in the firm. A similar confirmation is required in respect of the directors of a recognised body which is a company, or the members of a recognised body which is an LLP.

(iv)   A reporting accountant is not required to report on trivial breaches due to clerical errors or mistakes in book-keeping, provided that they have been rectified on discovery and the accountant is satisfied that no client suffered any loss as a result.

(v)   In many practices, clerical and book-keeping errors will arise. In the majority of cases these may be classified by the reporting accountant as trivial breaches. However, a "trivial breach" cannot be precisely defined. The amount involved, the nature of the breach, whether the breach is deliberate or accidental, how often the same breach has occurred, and the time outstanding before correction (especially the replacement of any shortage) are all factors which should be considered by the accountant before deciding whether a breach is trivial.

(vi)   The SRA receives a number of reports which are qualified only by reference to trivial breaches, but which show a significant difference between liabilities to clients and client money held in client and other accounts. An explanation for this difference, from either the accountant or the solicitor, must be given.

(vii)   Accountants' reports should be sent to the Information Directorate.

(viii) For direct reporting by the accountant to the SRA in cases of concern, see rule 38 and note (i) to that rule.

Rule 48 – Practices with two or more places of business

If a practice has two or more offices:

(a) separate reports may be delivered in respect of the different offices; and

(b) separate *accounting periods* may be adopted for different offices, provided that:

(i) separate reports are delivered;

(ii) every office is covered by a report delivered within six months of the end of its *accounting period*; and

(iii) there are no gaps between the *accounting periods* covered by successive reports for any particular office or offices.

Rule 49 – Waivers

The *SRA* may waive in writing in any particular case or cases any of the provisions of Part F of the rules, and may revoke any waiver.

Note

Applications for waivers should be made to the Information Directorate. In appropriate cases, solicitors may be granted a waiver of the obligation to deliver an accountant's report (see rule 35, and note (ix) to that rule). The circumstances in which a waiver of any other provision of Part F would be given must be extremely rare.

Part G – Commencement

Rule 50 – Commencement

The Solicitors' Accounts Rules 1998 took effect on 22 July 1998 and had to be implemented by 1 May 2000. They replaced the Solicitors' Accounts Rules 1991, the Solicitors' Accounts (Legal Aid Temporary Provision) Rule 1992 and the Accountant's Report Rules 1991.

Appendix 1 – Flowchart – effect of Solicitors' Accounts Rules 1998

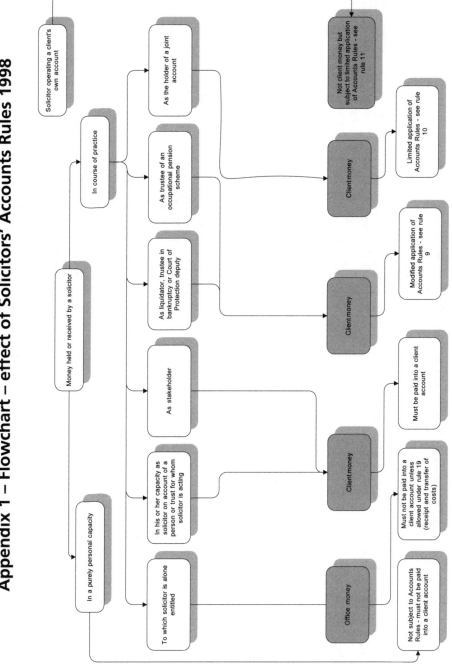

Appendix 2 – Special situations – what applies

	Is it client money?	Subject to reconciliations?	Keep books?	Retain statements?	Subject to accountant's report?	Produce records to SRA?	Interest?	Retain records generally?	Central records?	Subject to reporting accountant's comparisons?
1 R.16(1)(a) a/cs in solicitor's name (not client a/c)	Yes	Yes	Yes – r.32(1)(a) and 32(2)	Yes – r.32(9)	Yes	Yes	Yes – r.24	Yes – r.32(9)	Statements or register – r.32(11), bills – r.32(8)	Yes – r.42(1)(f)
2 R.16(1)(b) a/cs in name of client – not operated by solicitor	No	No	No – record solicitor's receipt and payment only	No	No	No	No – all interest earned for client – r.24, note (iii)	No – except record of solicitor's receipt and payment	Bills – r.32(8)	No
3 R.16(1)(b) a/cs in name of client – operated by solicitor	No	No	No – record solicitor's receipt and payment only	Yes – r.33	Limited – r.42(1)(n)	Yes – r.11	No – all interest earned for client – r.24, note (iii)	No – except record of solicitor's receipt and payment	Statements – r.33, Bills – r.32(8)	No
4 Liquidators, trustees in bankruptcy and Court of Protection deputies	Yes – r.9	No – r.9	Modified – statutory records – r.9	Yes – r.9 and r.32(9)(c)	Limited – r.42(1)(l)	Yes – r.9	No – r.9 – comply with statutory rules	Yes – modified r.32(9)(c)	Yes – r.32(12) Bills – r.32(8)	No – r.9
5 Trustees of occupational pension schemes	Yes – r.9	No – r.9	Modified – statutory records – r.9	Yes – r.9 and r.32(9)(c)	Limited – r.42(1)(l)	Yes – r.9	No – r.9 – comply with statutory rules	Yes – modified r.32(9)(c)	Yes – r.32(12) Bills – r.32(8)	No – r.9

6	Joint accounts – r.10	Yes – r.10	No – r.10	No – r.10	Yes – r.10 and 32(9)(b)(ii)	Limited – r.42(1)(m)	Yes – r.10	No. For joint a/c with client, all interest to client (r.24, note (ix)); for joint a/c with sol. depends on agreement	No – r.10	Statements – r.32(13); Bills – r.32(8)	No – r.10
7	Solicitor acting under power of attorney	Yes	Yes	Yes	Yes	Yes	Yes	Yes	Yes	Bills – r.32(8)	Yes
8	Solicitor operates client's own a/c e.g. under power of attorney – r.11	No	No	No	Yes – r.33	Limited – r.42(1)(n)	Yes – r.11	No – all interest earned for client (r.24, note (iii))	No – r.11	Statements – r.33; Bills – r.32(8)	No
9	Exempt solicitors under r.5	No	No	No	No	No	No	No	No	No	No

Appendix 3 – SRA guidelines – accounting procedures and systems

1. Introduction

1.1 These guidelines, published under rule 29 of the Solicitors' Accounts Rules 1998, are intended to be a benchmark or broad statement of good practice requirements which should be present in an effective regime for the proper control of client money. They should therefore be of positive assistance to firms in establishing or reviewing appropriate procedures and systems. They do not override, or detract from the need to comply fully with, the Accounts Rules.

1.2 References to partners or firms in the guidelines are intended to include sole practitioners, and recognised bodies and their managers.

2. General

2.1 Compliance with the Accounts Rules is the equal responsibility of all partners in a firm. They should establish policies and systems to ensure that the firm complies fully with the rules. Responsibility for day to day supervision may be delegated to one or more partners to enable effective control to be exercised. Delegation of total responsibility to a cashier or book-keeper is not acceptable.

2.2 The firm should hold a copy of the current version of the Solicitors' Accounts Rules and/or have ready access to the current on-line version. The person who maintains the books of account must have a full knowledge of the requirements of the rules and the accounting requirements of solicitors' firms.

2.3 Proper books of account should be maintained on the double-entry principle. They should be legible, up to date and contain narratives with the entries which identify and/or provide adequate information about the transaction. Entries should be made in chronological order and the current balance should be shown on client ledger accounts, or be readily ascertainable, in accordance with rule 32(5).

2.4 Ledger accounts for clients, other persons or trusts should include the name of the client or other person or trust and contain a heading which provides a description of the matter or transaction.

2.5 Separate designated client accounts should be brought within the ambit of the systems and procedures for the control of client money, including reconciliations (see 5.4 below).

2.6 Manual systems for recording client money are capable of complying with these guidelines and there is no requirement on firms to adopt computerised systems. A computer system, with suitable support procedures will, however, usually provide an efficient means of producing the accounts and associated control information.

2.7 If a computer system is introduced care must be taken to ensure:

(1) that balances transferred from the old books of account are reconciled

with the opening balances held on the new system before day to day operation commences;

(2) that the new system operates correctly before the old system is abandoned. This may require a period of parallel running of the old and new systems and the satisfactory reconciliation of the two sets of records before the old system ceases.

2.8 The firm should ensure that office account entries in relation to each client or trust matter are maintained up to date as well as the client account entries. Credit balances on office account in respect of client or trust matters should be fully investigated.

2.9 The firm should operate a system to identify promptly situations which may require the payment of interest to clients.

3. Receipt of client money

3.1 The firm should have procedures for identifying client money, including cash, when received in the firm, and for promptly recording the receipt of the money either in the books of account or a register for later posting to the client cash book and ledger accounts. The procedures should cover money received through the post, electronically or direct by fee earners or other personnel. They should also cover the safekeeping of money prior to payment to bank.

3.2 The firm should have a system which ensures that client money is paid promptly into a client account.

3.3 The firm should have a system for identifying money which should not be in a client account and for transferring it without delay.

3.4 The firm should determine a policy and operate a system for dealing with money which is a mixture of office money and client money, in compliance with rules 19–21.

4. Payments from client account

4.1 The firm should have clear procedures for ensuring that all withdrawals from client accounts are properly authorised. In particular, suitable persons, consistent with rule 23(1), should be named for the following purposes:

(1) authorisation of internal payment vouchers;

(2) signing client account cheques;

(3) authorising telegraphic or electronic transfers.

No other personnel should be allowed to authorise or sign the documents.

4.1A The firm should establish clear procedures and systems for ensuring that persons permitted to authorise the withdrawal of client money from a client account have an appropriate understanding of the requirements of the rules, including rules 22 and 23 which set out when and how a withdrawal from client account may properly be made.

4.2   Persons nominated for the purpose of authorising internal payment vouchers should, for each payment, ensure there is supporting evidence showing clearly the reason for the payment, and the date of it. Similarly, persons signing cheques and authorising transfers should ensure there is a suitable voucher or other supporting evidence to support the payment.

4.3   The firm should have a system for checking the balances on client ledger accounts to ensure no debit balances occur. Where payments are to be made other than out of cleared funds, clear policies and procedures must be in place to ensure that adequate risk assessment is applied.

N.B. If incoming payments are ultimately dishonoured, a debit balance will arise, in breach of the rules, and full replacement of the shortfall will be required under rule 7. See also rule 22, notes (v) and (vi).

4.4   The firm should establish systems for the transfer of costs from client account to office account in accordance with rule 19(2) and (3). Normally transfers should be made only on the basis of rendering a bill or written notification. The payment from the client account should be by way of a cheque or transfer in favour of the firm or sole principal – see rule 23(3).

4.5   The firm should establish policies and operate systems to control and record accurately any transfers between clients of the firm. Where these arise as a result of loans between clients, the written authority of both the lender and borrower must be obtained in accordance with rule 30(2).

4.6   The firm should establish policies and operate systems for the timely closure of files and the prompt accounting for surplus balances in accordance with rule 15(3).

4.7   The firm should establish systems in accordance with rule 15(4) to keep clients (or other people on whose behalf money is held) regularly informed when funds are retained for a specified reason at the end of a matter or the substantial conclusion of a matter.

5.   Overall control of client accounts

5.1   The firm should maintain control of all its bank and building society accounts opened for the purpose of holding client money. In the case of a joint account, a suitable degree of control should be exercised.

5.2   Central records or central registers must be kept in respect of:

(1)   accounts held for client money, which are not client accounts (rules 16(1) (a), 17(ca) and 32(11));

(2)   practice as a liquidator, trustee in bankruptcy, Court of Protection deputy or trustee of an occupational pension scheme (rules 9 and 32(12));

(3)   joint accounts (rules 10 and 32(13));

(4)   dividend payments received by an executor, trustee or nominee company as nominee (rules 31(2) and 32(14)); and

(5)   clients' own accounts (rules 11, 16(1)(b) and 33(2)).

5.3   In addition, there should be a master list of all:

- general client accounts;

- separate designated client accounts;

- accounts held in respect of 5.2 above; and

- office accounts.

The master list should show the current status of each account; e.g. currently in operation or closed with date of closure.

5.4   The firm should operate a system to ensure that accurate reconciliations of the client accounts are carried out at least every five weeks or, in the case of passbook-operated separate designated client accounts for money held by solicitor-trustees, every 14 weeks. In particular it should ensure that:

(1)   a full list of client ledger balances is produced. Any debit balances should be listed, fully investigated and rectified immediately. The total of any debit balances cannot be "netted off" against the total of credit balances;

(2)   a full list of unpresented cheques is produced;

(3)   a list of outstanding lodgements is produced;

(4)   formal statements are produced reconciling the client account cash book balances, aggregate client ledger balances and the client bank accounts. All unresolved differences must be investigated and, where appropriate, corrective action taken;

(5)   a partner checks the reconciliation statement and any corrective action, and ensures that enquiries are made into any unusual or apparently unsatisfactory items or still unresolved matters.

5.5   Where a computerised system is used, the firm should have clear policies, systems and procedures to control access to client accounts by determining the personnel who should have "write to" and "read only" access. Passwords should be held confidentially by designated personnel and changed regularly to maintain security. Access to the system should not unreasonably be restricted to a single person nor should more people than necessary be given access.

5.6   The firm should establish policies and systems for the retention of the accounting records to ensure:

- books of account, reconciliations, bills, bank statements and passbooks are kept for at least 6 years;

- paid cheques, digital images of paid cheques and other authorities for the withdrawal of money from a client account are kept for at least two years;

- other vouchers and internal expenditure authorisation documents relating directly to entries in the client account books are kept for at least two years.

5.7   The firm should ensure that unused client account cheques are stored securely to prevent unauthorised access. Blank cheques should not be pre-signed. Any cancelled cheques should be retained.

Appendix 4 – Reporting Accountant's Checklist

Name of practice	

Results of test checks:

1. For all client money	Were any breaches discovered? (Tick the appropriate column.)		If "yes" should breaches be noted in the accountant;'s report?		Cross reference to audit file documentation.
(a) Book-keeping system for every office:	Yes	No	Yes	No	
(i)	The accounting records satisfactorily distinguish client money from all other money dealt with by the firm.					
(ii)	A separate ledger account is maintained for each client and trust (excepting section (l) below) and the particulars of all client money received, held or paid on account of each client and trust, including funds held on separate designated deposits, or elsewhere, are recorded.					
(iii)	The client ledgers for clients and trusts show a current balance at all times, or the current balance is readily ascertainable.					
(iv)	A record of all bills of costs and written notifications has been maintained, which distinguishes profit costs from disbursements, either in the form of a central record or a file of copies of such bills.					
(b) Postings to ledger accounts and casts:	Yes	No	Yes	No	
(i)	Postings to ledger accounts for clients and trusts from records of receipts and payments are correct.					
(ii)	Casts of ledger accounts for clients and trusts and receipts and payments records are correct.					
(iii)	Postings have been recorded in chronological sequence with the date being that of the initiation of the transaction.					
(c) Receipts and payments of client money:	Yes	No	Yes	No	
(i)	Sample receipts and payments of client money as shown in bank and building society statements have been compared with the firm's records of receipts and payments of client money, and are correct.					

1. continued…..		Were any breaches discovered? (Tick the appropriate column.)		If "yes" should breaches be noted in the accountant;'s report?		Cross reference to audit file documentation.
(ii)	Sample paid cheques, or digital images of the front and back of sample paid cheques, have been obtained and details agreed to receipts and payment records.					
(d)	**System of recording costs and making transfers:**	Yes	No	Yes	No	
(i)	The firm's system of recording costs has been ascertained and is suitable.					
(ii)	Costs have been drawn only where required for or towards payment of the firm's costs where there has been sent to the client a bill of costs or other written notification of the amount of the costs.					
(e)	**Examination of documents for verification of transactions and entries in accounting records:**	Yes	No	Yes	No	
(i)	Make a test examination of a number of client and trust files.					
(ii)	All client and trust files requested for examination were made available.					
(iii)	The financial transactions as detailed on client and trust files and other documentation (including transfers from one ledger account to another) were valid and appropriately authorised in accordance with Parts A and B of the Solicitors' Accounts Rules 1998 (SAR).					
(iv)	The financial transactions evidenced by documents on the client and trust files were correctly recorded in the books of account in a manner complying with Part D SAR.					
(f)	**Extraction of client ledger balances for clients and trusts:**	Yes	No	Yes	No	
(i)	The extraction of client ledger balances for clients and trusts has been checked for no fewer than two separate dates in the period subject to this report.					
(ii)	The total liabilities to clients and trusts as shown by such ledger accounts has been compared to the cash account balance(s) at each of the separate dates selected in (f)(i) above and agreed.					
(iii)	The cash account balance(s) at each of the dates selected has/have been reconciled to the balance(s) in client bank account and elsewhere as confirmed directly by the relevant banks and building societies.					
(g)	**Reconciliations:**	Yes	No	Yes	No	
(i)	During the accounting year under review, reconciliations have been carried out at least every five weeks or, in the case of passbook-operated separate designated client accounts for money held by solicitor-trustees, every fourteen weeks.					
(ii)	Each reconciliation is in the form of a statement set out in a logical format which is likely to reveal any discrepancies.					
(iii)	Reconciliation statements have been retained.					
(iv)	On entries in an appropriate sample of reconciliation statements:	Yes	No	Yes	No	
	(A) All accounts containing client money have been included.					
	(B) All ledger account balances for clients and trusts as at the reconciliation date have been listed and totalled.					
	(C) No debit balances on ledger accounts for clients and trusts have been included in the total.					

1. continued…….		Were any breaches discovered? (Tick the appropriate column.)		If "yes" should breaches be noted in the accountant;'s report?		Cross reference to audit file documentation.
	(D) The cash account balance(s) for clients and trusts is/are correctly calculated by the accurate and up to date recording of transactions.					
	(E) The client bank account totals for clients and trusts are complete and correct being calculated by:					
	the closing balance **plus** an accurate and complete list of outstanding lodgements **less** an accurate and complete list of unpresented cheques.					
(v)	Each reconciliation selected under paragraph (iv) above has been achieved by the comparison and agreement **without adjusting or balancing entries** of:					
	total of ledger balances for clients and trusts;					
	total of cash account balances for clients and trusts;					
	total of client bank accounts.					
(vi)	In the event of debit balances existing on ledger accounts for clients and trusts, the firm has investigated promptly and corrected the position satisfactorily.					
(vii)	In the event of the reconciliations selected under paragraph (iv) above not being in agreement, the differences have been investigated and corrected promptly.					
(h)	**Payments of client money:**	Yes	No	Yes	No	
	Make a test examination of the ledger accounts for clients and trusts in order to ascertain whether payments have been made on any individual account in excess of money held on behalf of that client or trust.					
(i)	**Office accounts – client money:**	Yes	No	Yes	No	
(i)	Check such office ledger and cash account and bank and building society statements as the firm maintains with a view to ascertaining whether any client money has not been paid into a client account.					
(ii)	Investigate office ledger credit balances and ensure that such balances do not include client money incorrectly held in office account.					
(j)	**Client money not held in client account:**	Yes	No	Yes	No	
(i)	Have sums not held on client account been identified?					
(ii)	Has the reason for holding such sums outside client account been established?					
(iii)	Has a written client agreement been made if appropriate?					
(iv)	Are central records or a central register kept for client money held outside client account on the client's instructions?					
(k)	**Rule 30 – inter-client transfers:**	Yes	No	Yes	No	
	Make test checks of inter-client transfers to ensure that rule 30 has been complied with.					
(l)	**Rule 32(6) – acting for borrower and lender:**	Yes	No	Yes	No	
	Make a test examination of the client ledger accounts in order to ascertain whether rule 32(6) SAR has been complied with, where the firm acts for both borrower and lender in a conveyancing transaction.					
(m)	**Rule 32(14) – executor, trustee or nominee companies:**	Yes	No	Yes	No	
	Is a central book of dividend instruction letters kept?					

1. continued.......	Were any breaches discovered? (Tick the appropriate column.)		If "yes" should breaches be noted in the accountant;'s report?		Cross reference to audit file documentation.
(n) **Information and explanations:**	Yes	No	Yes	No	
All information and explanations required have been received and satisfactorily cleared.					

2. Liquidators, trustees in bankruptcy, Court of Protection deputies and trustees of occupational pension schemes (rule 9).	Were any breaches discovered? (Tick the appropriate column.)		If 'yes' should breaches be noted in the accountant's report?		Cross reference to audit file documentation
	Yes	No	Yes	No	
(a)	A record of all bills of costs and written notifications has been maintained which distinguishes profit costs from disbursements, either in the form of a central record or a file of copies of such bills or notifications.					
(b)	Records kept under rule 9 including any statements, passbooks and other accounting records originating outside the firm's office have been retained.					
(c)	Records kept under rule 9 are kept together centrally, or a central register is kept of the appointments.					

3. Joint accounts (rule 10)	Were any breaches discovered? (Tick the appropriate column.)		If 'yes' should breaches be noted in the accountant's report?		Cross reference to audit file documentation
	Yes	No	Yes	No	
(a)	A record of all bills of costs and written notifications has been maintained which distinguishes profit costs from disbursements, either in the form of a central record or a file of copies of such bills or notifications.					
(b)	Statements and passbooks and/or duplicate statements or copies of passbook entries have been retained.					
(c)	Statements, passbooks, duplicate statements and copies of passbook entries are kept together centrally, or a central register of all joint accounts is kept.					

4. Clients' own accounts (rule 11)	Were any breaches discovered? (Tick the appropriate column.)		If 'yes' should breaches be noted in the accountant's report?		Cross reference to audit file documentation
	Yes	No	Yes	No	
(a)	Statements and passbooks and/or duplicate statements, copies of passbook entries and cheque details have been retained.					
(b)	Statements and passbooks and/or duplicate statements, copies of passbook entries and cheque details are kept together centrally, or a central register of clients' own accounts is kept.					

5. SRA guidelines – accounting procedures and systems	Yes	No
Discovery of substantial departures from the guidelines? *If "yes" please give details below.*		

6. Please give further details of unsatisfactory items below. (Please attach additional schedules as required.)

Signature	Date
Reporting Accountant	Print Name

Appendix 5 – Accountant's Report Form

AR1

Accountant's Report Form

Under rule 35 of the Solicitors' Accounts Rules 1998 (SAR) an annual accountant's report is required from:

♦ a sole practitioner, if the practitioner or any of his or her employees have held or received client money, or operated a client's own account as signatory;

♦ a recognised body and its managers, if the recognised body or any of its managers or employees have held or received client money, or operated a client's own account as signatory;

♦ a solicitor or registered European lawyer (REL) in in-house practice who has held or received client money, or operated a client's own account as signatory, unless exempt under rule 5;

♦ a solicitor, REL or registered foreign lawyer (RFL) who was a manager or employee of a partnership which should have been a recognised body but was not, if the partnership or any of those managers or employees held or received client money, or operated a client's own account as signatory.

"Client money" in these notes and in the form includes controlled trust money held or received before 31 March 2009. As from 31 March 2009, that type of money is included in the definition of "client money".

A "recognised body" is a partnership, limited liability partnership (LLP) or company recognised by the SRA under section 9 of the Administration of Justice Act 1985. A "manager" is a partner in a partnership, a member of an LLP or a director of a company. In the case of a partnership, "manager" includes any person held out as a partner, including a "salaried partner", "associate partner" or "local partner". As from 1 July 2009 a sole practitioner has to be recognised by the SRA as a "recognised sole practitioner".

The managers and employees who, along with the recognised body, must be named on a recognised body's report, are those who are managers as at the date the report is signed by the accountant (or were managers as at the last date on which the report should have been delivered under rule 35, if the report is signed after that date) and, in addition:

♦ in the case of a partnership, any person who was a manager at any time during the report period, and any person who, as an employee during that period, held or received client money (e.g. as a named trustee) or operated a client's own account as signatory;

♦ in the case of an LLP or company, any person who, as a manager or employee during the report period, held or received client money (e.g. as a named trustee) or operated a client's own account as signatory.

The accountant who prepares the report must be qualified under rule 37 of the SAR and is required to report on compliance with Parts A and B, rule 24(1) of Part C, and Part D of the SAR.

When a practice ceases to hold and/or receive client money (and/or to operate any client's own account as signatory), either on closure of the practice or for any other reason, the practice must deliver a final report within six months of ceasing to hold and/or receive client money (and/or to operate any client's own account as signatory), unless the SRA requires earlier delivery.

When a practice closes but the ceased practice continues to hold or receive client money during the process of dealing with outstanding costs and unattributable or unreturnable funds, the SAR, including the obligation to deliver accountant's reports, will continue to apply. On ceasing to hold or receive client money, the ceased practice must deliver a final report within six months of ceasing to hold and/or receive client money, unless the SRA requires earlier delivery.

If you need any assistance completing this form please contact Information Services on 0870 606 2555 or by email at **contactcentre@sra.org.uk**. Our lines are open from 09.00 to 17.00 Monday to Friday. Please note calls may be monitored/recorded for training purposes.

If you are calling from overseas please use +44 (0) 1527 504450. Note that reports in respect of practice from an office outside England and Wales are submitted under rule 15.27 of the Solicitors' Code of Conduct 2007, and not under the SAR. Specimen form **AR2** may be used for such reports.

1

Revised May 2009

1 Firm details Insert here all names used by the firm or in-house practice in respect of practice from the offices covered by this report. This must include the registered name of a recognised body which is an LLP or company, and the name under which a partnership or sole practitioner is recognised.

Firm name(s) during the reporting period		SRA no	
Report Period from	to		

Is this the practice's final report?	Yes		No	

2 Firm's address(es) covered by this report All address(es) of the practice during the reporting period must be covered by an accountant's report, except those offices outside England and Wales not required under rule 15 of the Solicitors' Code of Conduct 2007 to deliver a report.

Address(es)

Office Type (Head office / branch office)	Office Type (Head office / branch office)

PLEASE COMPLETE ONE ONLY OF SECTIONS 3A, 3B, 3C AND 3D AS APPROPRIATE.

3A Sole practice. Please list the name of the sole practitioner and any consultant or employee who held or received client money, or operated a client's own account as signatory, during the report period.

Surname	Initials	SRA No.	Category – sole solicitor, sole REL, consultant, employee

2

3B Recognised body (partnership). Please list the names of all the "managers", whether individuals or bodies corporate, at the relevant date (date report is signed or due date for delivery); and any person who was a "manager" at any time during the report period; and any consultant or employee who held or received client money (e.g. as a named trustee), or operated a client's own account as signatory, during the report period; (see introductory notes).

Surname or corporate name	Initials	SRA No.	Category – manager, corporate manager, consultant, employee	Quote date if ceased to hold or receive client money

3

3C Recognised body (LLP or company). Please list the names of all the "managers", whether individuals or bodies corporate, at the relevant date (date report is signed or due date for delivery); and any "manager", consultant or employee who held or received client money (e.g. as a named trustee), or operated a client's own account as signatory, during the report period; (see introductory notes).

Surname or corporate name	Initials	SRA No.	Category – manager, corporate manager, consultant, employee

3D In-house practice. Please list the name of every principal solicitor / REL who held or received client money at any time during the report period.

Surname	Initials	SRA No.	Category – solicitor, REL	Quote date if ceased to hold or receive client money

4

4 Comparison dates

The results of the comparisons required under rule 42(1)(f) of the Solicitors' Accounts Rules 1998, at the dates selected by me/us were:

(a)   at   [   ]   *(insert date 1)*

    (i)   Liabilities to clients and trusts (and other persons for whom client money is held) as shown by   £ [   ]
ledger accounts for client and trust matters.

    (ii) Cash held in client account, and client money held in any account other than a client account, after £ [   ]
allowances for lodgments cleared after date and for outstanding cheques.

    (iii) Difference between (i) and (ii) (if any).   £ [   ]

(b)   at   [   ]   *(insert date 2)*

    (i)   Liabilities to clients and trusts (and other persons for whom client money is held) as shown by   £ [   ]
ledger accounts for client and trust matters.

    (ii) Cash held in client account, and client money held in any account other than a client account, after £ [   ]
allowances for lodgments cleared after date and for outstanding cheques.

    (iii) Difference between (i) and (ii) (if any).   £ [   ]

Notes:

The figure to be shown in 4(a)(i) and 4(b)(i) above is the total of credit balances, without adjustment for debit balances (unless capable of proper set off, i.e. being in respect of the same client), or for receipts and payments not capable of allocation to individual ledger accounts.

An explanation must be given for any significant difference shown at 4(a)(iii) or 4(b)(iii) - see note (vi) to rule 47 of Solicitors' Accounts Rules 1998. If appropriate, it would be helpful if the explanation is given here.

5

5 Qualified report

Have you found it necessary to make this report 'Qualified'?   No ☐   If "No" proceed to section 6

                                                                      Yes ☐   If "Yes" please complete the
                                                                              relevant boxes

(a) Please indicate in the space provided any matters (other than trivial breaches) in respect of which it appears to you that there has been
     a failure to comply with the provisions of Parts A and B, rule 24(1) of Part C, and Part D of the Solicitors' Accounts Rules 1998 and, in
     the case of private practice only, any part of the period covered by this report for which the practice does not appear to have been
     covered in respect of its offices in England and Wales by the insurance/indemnity documents referred to in rule 42(1)(p) of the Solicitors'
     Accounts Rules 1998 *(continue on an additional sheet if necessary)*:

(b) Please indicate in the space provided any matters in respect of which you have been unable to satisfy yourself and the reasons for
     that inability, e.g. because a client's file is not available *(continue on an additional sheet if necessary)*.

6 Accountant details The reporting accountant must be qualified in accordance with rule 37 of the Solicitors' Accounts Rules 1998.

Name of accountant		Professional body	
		Accountant membership/ registration number	
Recognised Supervisory Body under which individual/firm is a registered auditor		Reference number of individual/firm audit registration(s)	
Firm name			
Firm address			

6

7 Declaration

In compliance with Part F of the Solicitors' Accounts Rules 1998, I/we have examined to the extent required by rule 42 of those rules, the accounting records, files and other documents produced to me/us in respect of the above practice.

In so far as an opinion can be based on this limited examination, I am/we are satisfied that during the above mentioned period the practice has complied with the provisions of Parts A and B, rule 24(1) of Part C, and Part D of the Solicitors' Accounts Rules 1998 except so far as concerns:

    (i)   certain trivial breaches due to clerical errors or mistakes in book-keeping, all of which were rectified on discovery and none of which, I am/we are satisfied, resulted in any loss to any client or trust; and/or

    (ii)   any matters detailed in section 5 of this report.

In the case of private practice only, I/we certify that, in so far as can be ascertained from a limited examination of the insurance/indemnity documents produced to me/us, the practice was covered in respect of its offices in England and Wales for the period covered by this report by the insurance/indemnity documents referred to in rule 42(1)(p) of the Solicitors' Accounts Rules 1998, except as stated in section 5 of this report.

I/we have relied on the exception contained in rule 42(2) of the Solicitors' Accounts Rules 1998.   Yes

---

Rule 42(2) of the Solicitors' Accounts Rules 1998 states: "For the purposes of paragraph(1)(f) above [extraction of balances] if a solicitor uses a computerised or mechanised system of accounting which automatically produces an extraction of all client ledger balances, the accountant need not check all client ledger balances extracted on the list produced by the computer or machine against the individual records of client ledger accounts, provided the accountant:

(a)   confirms that a satisfactory system of control is in operation and the accounting records are in balance;

(b)   carries out a test check of the extraction against the individual records; and

(c)   specifies in the report that he or she has relied on this exception."

In carrying out work in preparation of this report, I/we have discovered the following substantial departures from the SRA's current Guidelines for Accounting Procedures and Systems (*continue on an additional sheet if necessary*):

7

Please tick the "Yes" or "No" box for the following items (i) to (v) to show whether, so far as you are aware, the relevant statement applies in respect of yourself or any principal, director (in the case of a company), member (in the case of an LLP) or employee of your accountancy practice. *Give details if appropriate.*

		Yes	No
(i)	Any of the parties mentioned above is related to any solicitor(s)/REL(s)/RFL(s) or other manager(s) to whom this report relates.		

		Yes	No
(ii)	Any of the parties mentioned above normally maintained, on a regular basis, the accounting records to which this report relates.		

		Yes	No
(iii)	Any of the parties mentioned above, or the practice, places substantial reliance for referral of clients on the practice to which this report relates.		

		Yes	No
(iv)	Any of the parties mentioned above, or the practice, is a client or former client of the practice to which this report relates.		

		Yes	No
(v)	There are other circumstances which might affect my independence in preparing this report.		

The information is intended to help the SRA to identify circumstances which might make it difficult to give an independent report. Answering "Yes" to any part of this section does not disqualify the accountant from making the report.

Information within the accountant's personal knowledge should always be disclosed. Detailed investigations are not necessary but reasonable enquiries should be made of those directly involved in the work.

8

I/we have completed and signed the checklist and retained a copy. The original checklist has been sent to either each of the persons listed in Section 3 or to one of them on behalf of them all.

I/we confirm that a copy of this report has been sent to (* delete as appropriate):

(a)   * Each of the persons listed in Section 3; or

(b)   * The following manager in the recognised body, on behalf of all the managers in the recognised body:

_____

The form should then be signed and dated. The report can be signed in the name of the firm of accountants of which the accountant is a partner (in the case of a partnership) or director (in the case of a company) or member (in the case of an LLP) or employee. Particulars of the individual accountant signing the report must be given in section 6.

Please note that if this report is not completed by an accountant with the qualifications required under rule 37 of the Solicitors' Accounts Rules 1998 it will not be accepted and will be returned to the firm for which the report has been submitted.

Date	

Signature	

Name (Block Capitals)	

Please return this form to: Information Directorate
                               Solicitors Regulation Authority
                               Ipsley Court
                               Berrington Close
                               Redditch
                               Worcestershire
                               B98 0TD

                OR   DX 19114 Redditch

The reporting accountant's checklist should be retained by the legal practice for at least three years, and not submitted with this report.

9

Index

This index does not form part of the rules.

References are to the numbers of the Rules. An 'n' after the Rule number refers to one of the notes appended to that Rule. References to the appendices are prefaced by 'app'.

Solicitors Disciplinary Tribunal
  misconduct by employee of a solicitor, 4n(i)
  report used in proceedings, 34(7)
Solicitors Regulation Authority
  authorisation of withdrawal from client account, 22(1)(h), 22n(viii)–(ix)
  authority to withhold money from client account, 17(f), 17n(iv)
  co-operation with checking compliance with rules, 1(h)
  guidelines for accounting systems, 29, app.3
  intervention, money in practice, 13n(viii)
  investigation powers, 34, 34n(ii)–(iv)
  meaning, 2(2)(xc)
  monitoring of compliance, 34, 34n(iii)
  reports from accountants to, 38(1)(i) and (iii), 38n(i)
Solicitor's rights, against money in client account, 12
Special situations chart, app.2
Spent, meaning, 22n(ii)
SRA *see* Solicitors Regulation Authority
Stakeholder
  administrative charges, 27n(ii)–(iv)
  contracting out of interest rules, 27(2), 27n(ii)–(v)
  holding client money, 13n(i)(a), app.1
  interest, 26
Stamp duty land tax
  client money, 13n(i)(c)
  included with payment of costs, 19(1)(a)(iii)
Standard monthly payments from Legal Services Commission, legal aid practitioners, 21(2), 21n(vii)–(x)
Standard terms of business
  client money held outside client account, 16(2)
  contracting out by, 27n(i)
Statutory rules
  accounting records, 9, 32(9)(c), 32(12), 32(15)(b), 32n(ii)(a)
  interest, 24n(viii)
Statutory undertakers
  exempt from rules, 5(a)(ii)
  meaning, 5n(i)
Stocks
  checks not required in accountant's reports, 44(b)
  purchase and sale, 15n(vii)
Successive accounts, amount of interest, 25(3)

Sum in lieu of interest, 24(2)–(5), 24(6)(b)
  amount of interest, 25
  checks not required by reporting accountant, 44(d)
  payment into client account, 15(2)(d)
  relevant period, 25(2), 25n(i)–(ii)
  stakeholder money, 26
  when to account to client, 25n(i)
Surveyors, fees, 2n(v)
Suspense ledger accounts, 32(16)
Taxi fares, 19n(ii), 22n(ii)
Telegraphic transfer
  calculation of interest, 25n(iii)
  for payment of costs, 19n(vi)–(viii)
  not received, 22n(vi)
Telegraphic transfer fees
  client money, 13n(i)(c)
  included with payment of costs, 19(1)(a)(iii)
Telephone instructions, withdrawal from client account, 23n(i)
Test procedures, accountant's reports, 42
Third parties, payments to legal aid practitioners, 21(3), 21n(iv)–(v)
Third party operation of joint account, 10(1), 10(3), 10(4)
Time of accounting
  for client money, no longer any proper reason to retain, 15(3)
  sum in lieu of interest, 25n(i)
Time of delivery, accountant's reports, 35(1), 36(5), 36n(ii)
Titles, client accounts, 14(3), 14n(ii), 14n(v)
Total liabilities to clients, 32(7), 42(1)(f)
  netting off of debits and credits not allowed, 32(n)(x), 42n(ii)
Transactions, small number of, waiver of accountant's reports, 35n(ix), 49
Transfers between client accounts, 22(1)(d)
Transfers between general client accounts, 23(2)
Transfers between clients
  general client account, 30(1)
  private loans, 30(2)
Transfers of costs, 19(3)
Translators, fees, 2n(v)
Travel agents, charges, 2n(v), 19n(ii)
Tribunal *see* Solicitors Disciplinary Tribunal
Trivial breaches, 47n(iv)–(v)
  alleged, but showing significant differences, 47n(vi)
Trust
  accounting records, 32

Part 2

Solicitors' Code of Conduct 2007 [extracts]

[with consolidated amendments to 31 March 2009]

Client relations

2.06 Commissions

If you are a recognised body, a manager of a recognised body or a recognised sole practitioner, you must ensure that your firm pays to your client commission received over £20 unless the client, having been told the amount, or if the precise amount is not known, an approximate amount or how the amount is to be calculated, has agreed that your firm may keep it.

Guidance to rule 2

Commissions – 2.06

52. Rule 2.06 reflects the legal position, preventing a solicitor making a secret profit arising from the solicitor–client relationship.

53. A commission:

   (a) is a financial benefit you receive by reason of and in the course of the relationship of solicitor and client; and

   (b) arises in the context that you have put a third party and the client in touch with one another. (See *The Law Society v Mark Hedley Adcock and Neil Kenneth Mocroft* [2006] EWHC 3212 (Admin).)

54. Examples of what amounts to a commission include payments received from a stockbroker on the purchase of stocks and shares, from an insurance company or an intermediary on the purchase or renewal of an insurance policy, and from a bank or building society on the opening of a bank account. Also, a payment made to you for introducing a client to a third party (unless the introduction was unconnected with any particular matter which you were currently or had been handling for the client) amounts to a commission.

55. On the other hand, a discount on a product or a rebate on, for example, a search fee would not amount to a commission because it does not arise

in the context of referring your client to a third party. Such payments are disbursements and the client must get the benefit of any discount or rebate.

56. A client can give informed consent only if you:

(a) provide details concerning the amount; and

(b) make it clear that they can withhold their consent and, if so, the commission will belong to them when it is received by you.

57. Commission received may be retained only if the conditions within 2.06 are complied with and the arrangement is in your client's best interests – either:

(a) it is used to offset a bill of costs; or

(b) you must be able to justify its retention – for example, the commission is retained in lieu of costs which you could have billed for work done in placing the business, but were not so billed.

58. It cannot be in the best interests of the client for you to receive the commission as a gift. There must be proper and fair legal consideration, such as your agreement to undertake legal work. In consequence, except where the commission is to be offset against a bill of costs:

(a) it is important that consent is obtained prior to the receipt of the commission (and preferably before you undertake the work leading to the paying of the commission);

(b) for the purposes of complying with 2.06 you may not obtain your client's consent to retain the commission after you have received it. If consent is not given beforehand, there can be no legal consideration and so the money belongs to the client; and

(c) if you have obtained consent but the amount actually received is materially in excess of the estimate given to your client, you cannot retrospectively obtain consent to retain the excess. The excess belongs to your client and should be handled accordingly.

59. In order to minimise possible confusion and misunderstanding, and to protect both you and your client, it is recommended that the agreement containing the details about the commission be in writing.

60. If it is your intention from the outset to use the commission to offset a bill of costs, it should be (subject to there being no specific instructions concerning the use of the commission):

(a) paid into client account as money on account of costs, if received before the bill has been submitted; or

(b) paid straight into office account if the bill has already been submitted.

61.   Where you intend to retain the commission in lieu of costs and your client has provided their consent in accordance with 2.06, the money may be paid into office account as soon as it is received. Where you have requested your client's consent and it has been refused, the commission will belong to the client on receipt and must be paid into client account. It may then be paid to the client or used to offset a bill subject to note 60 above. See the Solicitors' Accounts Rules 1998 for more information.

62.   Where you are a sole trustee or attorney or a joint trustee or attorney only with other solicitors, you cannot give proper consent to your retaining commission by purporting to switch capacities. Furthermore, you are very likely to be acting contrary to your fiduciary obligations at law.

63.   For further information about dealing with commission see the Solicitors' Financial Services (Scope) Rules 2001.

Business management in England and Wales

5.01 Supervision and management responsibilities

(1)   If you are a recognised body, a manager of a recognised body or a recognised sole practitioner, you must make arrangements for the effective management of the firm as a whole, and in particular provide for:

...

(c)   compliance by the firm and individuals with key regulatory requirements such as certification, registration or recognition by the Solicitors Regulation Authority, compulsory professional indemnity cover, delivery of accountants' reports, and obligations to co-operate with and report information to the Authority;

...

(g)   the safekeeping of documents and assets entrusted to the firm;

...

(j)   financial control of budgets, expenditure and cashflow;

Guidance to rule 5

Guidance on 5.01 generally

...

5.   Firms will be expected to be able to produce evidence of a systematic and effective approach to management, and this may include the implementation by the firm of one or more of the following:

...

(d) the guidelines for accounting procedures and systems published as Appendix 3 to the Solicitors' Accounts Rules 1998;

...

Compliance with key regulatory obligations – 5.01(1)(c)

15. The purpose of 5.01(1)(c) is to foster collective responsibility for the governance of the firm by requiring you to establish arrangements which provide for compliance with key regulatory obligations. These include arrangements to ensure that:

    ...

    (i) an accountant's report is delivered in accordance with the Solicitors' Accounts Rules; ...

17. If you are a sole practitioner or a manager in a firm then you are personally responsible for complying with the Solicitors' Accounts Rules, including the delivery of an annual accountant's report. You will be liable to disciplinary action if there is a failure to comply with those rules, even if you have delegated book-keeping to someone else in the firm. The nature of the disciplinary action will depend on the seriousness of the breach and the extent to which you knew or should have known of the breach. Similarly, in the case of a partnership or body corporate, the recognised body itself is directly responsible for complying with the Solicitors' Accounts Rules, including delivering an accountant's report, and is itself liable to disciplinary action.

18. If you are an in-house solicitor or in-house REL and you receive or hold client money you must comply with the Solicitors' Accounts Rules and must submit an accountant's report.

...

Safekeeping of documents and assets – 5.01(1)(g)

22. The terms "documents" and "assets" should be interpreted in a non-technical way to include, for example, client money, wills, deeds, investments and other property entrusted to the firm by clients and others.

23. The detail of the firm's arrangements will be a matter for you to decide in all the circumstances. However, as a minimum requirement you must be able to identify to whom documents and assets belong, and in connection with which matter.

...

Financial control of budgets, expenditure and cashflow – 5.01(1)(j)

31. Client money is more likely to be at risk in a firm where the recognised

body and its managers, or the recognised sole practitioner, do not exercise adequate oversight of the firm's own financial arrangements. The purpose of 5.01(1)(j) is to ensure this is addressed in the overall management framework – not to prescribe particular financial systems or to prevent you from delegating day-to-day financial operations to suitable staff. It may also help firms to ensure that they are looking forward when undertaking their financial management, so that they will know they will be able to cover their commitments and plan their resources properly. It should be noted, however, that some accounting and management information systems do not assist in this regard, as they tend to deal only with historic information.

Continuation of the practice of the firm in the event of absences and emergencies, etc. – 5.01(1)(k)

...

33. If you are away for a month or more, and you are the only person in the firm "qualified to supervise" under 5.02, the arrangements for complying with 5.01(1)(k) will normally need to include the provision of another person qualified to supervise.

34. Rule 23 of the Solicitors' Accounts Rules requires that a withdrawal from a client account cannot be made without a specific authority. This rule cannot be complied with if blank cheques are left for completion by staff at a later date, as signing a blank cheque is not giving a specific authority.

35. If you have not made adequate arrangements in advance to meet unforeseen circumstances, difficulties may arise in the conduct of clients' affairs and in the administration of your own business. For example, a client may attend the office asking for urgent assistance, an accountant's report must be submitted, a practising certificate must be applied for or indemnity cover must be obtained notwithstanding your absence. Consequently, if you are a sole practitioner or sole director, you should have an arrangement with another solicitor or REL (sufficiently experienced and entitled to practise) to supervise your firm until you return. You should notify your bank of these arrangements in advance, so that the solicitor or REL covering your absence can operate your client and office accounts.

...

Publicity

Guidance to rule 7

Salaried partners

35. A manager who is held out on the letterhead of an unincorporated firm as a

partner – even if separately designated as a "salaried" or "associate" partner – is treated by the SRA as a full partner and manager, and therefore must comply with the Solicitors' Accounts Rules and the Solicitors' Indemnity Insurance Rules. Holding out as a partner someone who is not entitled under rule 14 to be a partner will put you and your firm in breach both of rule 7 and rule 14.

In-house practice, etc.

Guidance to rule 13

Accounts rules and accountants' reports

10. If you are an in-house solicitor or in-house REL employed in England and Wales, and you receive or hold clients' money, you must comply with the Solicitors' Accounts Rules 1998. If you pay in or endorse over a cheque made out in your favour, you receive clients' money and must deal with it in accordance with the relevant rules (see note (viii) to rule 35 of the Solicitors' Accounts Rules 1998). For the name of a client account, see rule 14(3) of the Solicitors' Accounts Rules 1998. Even if a cheque is simply endorsed over to your employer, you will need to keep a record (see rule 32 of the Solicitors' Accounts Rules 1998), submit an accountant's report, and pay the full contribution to the Compensation Fund. If you receive only your employer's money you can try to ensure that all cheques are made payable to the employer. If you are an in-house solicitor or in-house REL employed overseas, the Solicitors' Accounts Rules do not apply but you must comply with similar requirements which are set out in 15.27.

11. An in-house accountant (working for the same employer) may not prepare an accountant's report for an in-house solicitor or in-house REL (see rule 37(2)(a) of the Solicitors' Accounts Rules 1998).

12. If you only undertake a small number of transactions or handle a small volume of clients' money in a year, you can apply to the Caseworking and Applications department of the SRA for a dispensation from the obligation to deliver an accountant's report. However, dispensations are not given as a matter of course.

13. If you are:

    (a) a solicitor or REL practising as an employee of:

        (i) a local authority;

        (ii) statutory undertakers;

        (iii) a body whose accounts are audited by the Comptroller and Auditor General;

      (iv) the Duchy of Lancaster;

      (v)   the Duchy of Cornwall; or

      (vi) the Church Commissioners;

(b)   a solicitor practising as the Solicitor of the City of London; or

(c)   a solicitor or REL carrying out the functions of:

      (i)   a coroner or other judicial office; or

      (ii) a sheriff or under-sheriff,

you need not comply with the Solicitors' Accounts Rules 1998 (see rule 5 of those rules) or submit an accountant's report. However, if you hold or receive client money, you must pay the full Compensation Fund contribution, but this will not apply if you come within note 13(c) and are not practising as a solicitor.

Separate practice through a firm

...

17.   If you hold or receive client money as a manager in a firm in England and Wales you must comply with the Solicitors' Accounts Rules 1998.

...

Recognised bodies

Guidance to rule 14

Compliance with rules

22.   In addition to these rules, a recognised body must comply with the Solicitors' Indemnity Insurance Rules, the Solicitors' Accounts Rules and (unless authorised by the FSA) with the Solicitors' Financial Services (Scope) Rules and the Solicitors' Financial Services (Conduct of Business) Rules.

(a)   Indemnity insurance

23.   The Solicitors' Indemnity Insurance Rules require a recognised body to have "qualifying insurance" from a "qualifying insurer" (with some limited scope for exemptions in respect of RELs' participation in recognised bodies). The basic minimum level of cover is £2 million for any one claim. A recognised body with limited liability (i.e. an LLP, a limited company, or a partnership one or more of whose partners is an LLP or a limited company) is required to have minimum cover of £3 million for any one claim. Some recognised bodies which are nominee companies escape the requirement for an extra

£1 million cover – see note 28(d) below. A recognised body may also have additional "top-up" cover, from any insurer.

(b) Accountants' reports

24. If a recognised body holds or receives client money, it will in due course have to deliver an accountant's report to the SRA. This obligation also extends to the "managers" of the recognised body. The names of the current "managers" along with the name of the recognised body must appear on the accountant's report, as well as the name of any employee or "manager" who or which has held or received client money, and any individual employee or "manager" who has operated a client's own account as signatory.

Executor, trustee and nominee companies

...

28. In relation to an English executor, trustee or nominee company, you should also note that:

(a) a recognised body, when holding money or receiving dividends as nominee, holds client money, and it must have its own client account, in its own name;

(b) a single set of accounting records may be used for the company and the main practice and a single accountant's report can be delivered for both, if the relevant accounting periods are the same, and provided the accountant deals with the accounts for each separately;

(c) a wholly owned executor, trustee or nominee company can be covered by the same policy of qualifying insurance as your main practice, but only if the company is named on the policy and certificate of insurance as a separate insured; and

(d) a nominee company may be exempt from the requirement to have an extra £1 million qualifying insurance if it can show that:

(i)   it is a nominee company only;

(ii) all the directors of the company are partners or members in your main practice;

(iii) it holds assets only for clients of your main practice;

(iv) it can act only as agent for your main practice; and

(v)   all fees accrue to the benefit of your main practice.

Overseas practice

15.01 Core duties (rule 1) application, and conflicts of rules

General application of these rules to overseas practice

(2) (a) Subject to (3) and (4) below, these rules apply, in relation to practice from an office outside the UK:

    (i) to a solicitor as an individual, whether or not the solicitor's firm or employer is subject to these rules;

    (ii) to a solicitor-controlled recognised body (as defined in rule 24); and

    (iii) to a lawyer of England and Wales other than a solicitor, and to a non-lawyer, in relation to practice as a manager of a solicitor-controlled recognised body,

    and notwithstanding the application of the rules to its solicitor managers and solicitor employees, a recognised body which is not a solicitor-controlled recognised body is not itself subject to these rules in relation to practice from such an office.

  (b) Subject to (3) and (4) below, these rules apply, in relation to practice from an office in Scotland or Northern Ireland:

    (i) to a solicitor or REL as an individual, whether or not the solicitor's or REL's firm or employer is subject to these rules;

    (ii) to a solicitor-controlled recognised body;

    (iii) to an REL-controlled recognised body (as defined in rule 24);

    (iv) to a lawyer of England and Wales other than a solicitor, to a European lawyer registered with the Bar Standards Board and to a non-lawyer, in relation to practice as a manager of a solicitor-controlled recognised body or an REL-controlled recognised body; and

    (v) a solicitor who was formerly an REL, when practising as a lawyer of an Establishment Directive profession,

    and notwithstanding the application of the rules to its solicitor and REL managers and its solicitor and REL employees, a recognised body which is not a solicitor-controlled recognised body or an REL-controlled recognised body is not itself subject to these rules in relation to practice from such an office.

Modification of these rules in relation to overseas practice

(3) If this rule states that a rule or a provision of these rules does not apply to your overseas practice, you may disregard that rule or provision in relation to your overseas practice, but you must comply with any alternative provision which is substituted by this rule.

(4) If compliance with any applicable provision of these rules would result in your breaching local law, you may disregard that provision to the extent necessary to comply with that local law.

15.15 Deposit interest

(1) You must comply with (2) below, if you are:

   (a) a solicitor sole practitioner practising from an office outside England and Wales, or an REL sole practitioner practising from an office in Scotland or Northern Ireland;

   (b) a solicitor-controlled recognised body or (in relation to practice from an office in Scotland or Northern Ireland) a solicitor-controlled recognised body or an REL-controlled recognised body;

   (c) a solicitor manager of a firm which is practising from an office outside the UK, and solicitors control the firm, either directly as partners, members or owners, or indirectly by their ownership of bodies corporate which are partners, members or owners; or

   (d) a solicitor or REL manager of a firm which is practising from an office in Scotland or Northern Ireland, and solicitors and/or RELs control the firm, either directly as partners, members or owners, or indirectly by their ownership of bodies corporate which are partners, members or owners.

(2) If interest ought, in fairness, to be earned for the client on client money held under (1) above, you must ensure that:

   (a) the client money is dealt with so that proper interest is earned upon it, and that the interest is paid to the client;

   (b) the client is paid a sum equivalent to the interest that would have been earned if the client money had earned proper interest; or

   (c) any alternative written agreement with the client setting out arrangements regarding the payment of interest on that money is carried out.

(3) In deciding whether interest ought, in fairness, to be earned for a client on client money, you must have regard to all the circumstances, including:

   (a) the amount of the money;

   (b) the length of time for which you are likely to hold the money; and

   (c) the law and prevailing custom of lawyers practising in the jurisdiction in which you are practising.

15.27 Accounts

Practice from an office outside the UK

(1) You must comply with (3) and (4) below in relation to practice from an office outside the UK if you are:

(a)   a solicitor sole practitioner who has held or received client money;

(b)   a solicitor-controlled recognised body which has held or received client money as a firm;

(c)   a lawyer of England and Wales, or a non-lawyer, who is a manager of a solicitor-controlled recognised body which holds or receives client money;

(d)   a solicitor manager of any other firm which is controlled by solicitors, either directly as partners, members or owners, or indirectly by their ownership of bodies corporate which are partners, members or owners, if the firm holds or receives client money;

(e)   a solicitor who holds or receives client money as a named trustee;

(f)   a lawyer of England and Wales, or a non-lawyer, who is a manager of a solicitor-controlled recognised body and who holds or receives client money as a named trustee.

Practice from an office in Scotland or Northern Ireland

(2)   You must comply with (3) and (4) below in relation to practice from an office in Scotland or Northern Ireland if you are:

(a)   a solicitor or REL sole practitioner who has held or received client money;

(b)   a solicitor-controlled recognised body or an REL-controlled recognised body which has held or received client money as a firm;

(c)   a lawyer of England and Wales, an REL, a European lawyer registered with the Bar Standards Board or a non-lawyer, who is a manager of a solicitor-controlled recognised body, or an REL-controlled recognised body, which holds or receives client money;

(d)   a solicitor or REL manager of any other firm which is controlled by solicitors and/or RELs, either directly as partners, members or owners, or indirectly by their ownership of bodies corporate which are partners, members or owners, if the firm holds or receives client money;

(e)   a solicitor or REL who holds or receives client money as a named trustee;

(f)   a lawyer of England and Wales, a European lawyer registered with the Bar Standards Board or a non-lawyer, who is a manager of a solicitor-controlled recognised body or an REL-controlled recognised body and who holds or receives client money as a named trustee.

Dealings with client money

(3)   In all dealings with client money, you must ensure that:

(a)   it is kept in a client account separate from money which is not client money;

(b)   on receipt, it is paid without delay into a client account and kept there, unless the client has expressly or by implication agreed that the money shall be dealt with otherwise or you pay it straight over to a third party in the execution of a trust under which it is held;

(c) it is not paid or withdrawn from a client account except:

(i) on the specific authority of the client;

(ii) where the payment or withdrawal is properly required:

(A) for a payment to or on behalf of the client;

(B) for or towards payment of a debt due to the firm from the client or in reimbursement of money expended by the firm on behalf of the client; or

(C) for or towards payment of costs due to the firm from the client, provided that a bill of costs or other written intimation of the amount of the costs incurred has been delivered to the client and it has thereby (or otherwise in writing) been made clear to the client that the money held will be applied in payment of the costs due; or

(iii) in proper execution of a trust under which it is held;

(d) accounts are kept at all times, whether by written, electronic, mechanical or other means, to:

(i) record all dealings with client money in any client account;

(ii) show all client money received, held or paid, distinct from any other money, and separately in respect of each client or trust; and

(iii) ensure that the firm is able at all times to account, without delay, to each and every client or trust for all money received, held or paid on behalf of that client or trust; and

(e) all accounts, books, ledgers and records kept in relation to the firm's client account(s) are preserved for at least six years from the date of the last entry therein.

Accountants' reports

(4) (a) You must deliver an accountant's report in respect of any period during which you or your firm have held or received client money and you were subject to (3) above.

(b) The accountant's report must be signed by the reporting accountant, who must be an accountant qualified in England and Wales or in the overseas jurisdiction where your office is based, or by such other person as the Solicitors Regulation Authority may think fit. The Authority may for reasonable cause disqualify a person from signing accountants' reports.

(c) The accountant's report must be based on a sufficient examination of the relevant documents to give the reporting accountant a reasonable indication whether or not you have complied with (3) above during the period covered by the report, and must include the following:

(i) your name, practising address(es) and practising style and the name(s) of the firm's managers;

(ii) the name, address and qualification of the reporting accountant;

(iii) an indication of the nature and extent of the examination the reporting accountant has made of the relevant documents;

(iv) a statement of the total amount of money held at banks or similar institutions on behalf of clients and trusts, and of the total liabilities to clients and trusts, on any date selected by the reporting accountant (including the last day), falling within the period under review; and an explanation of any difference between the total amount of money held for clients and trusts and the total liabilities to clients and trusts;

(v) if the reporting accountant is satisfied that (so far as may be ascertained from the examination) you have complied with (3) above during the period covered by the report, except for trivial breaches, or situations where you have been bound by a local rule not to comply, a statement to that effect; and

(vi) if the reporting accountant is not sufficiently satisfied to give a statement under (v) above, details of any matters in respect of which it appears to the reporting accountant that you have not complied with (3) above.

Guidance to rule 15

Conflicts of rules – 15.01(4)

8. A conflict of rules can arise when you are required to comply with two sets of rules, but if you comply with one you will breach the other. This situation can arise when:

   (a) you are practising in another jurisdiction and you are required by local or EU legislation to comply with the rules of the local legal profession – for instance, you are a solicitor registered in another jurisdiction under the Establishment Directive, and there is a conflict between one of the local rules and one of the solicitors' rules; or

   (b) you are practising under dual title, e.g. as a solicitor and as a New York attorney, and a rule of the New York Bar conflicts with one of the solicitors' rules.

9. If a local rule applies, you cannot choose to comply only with that rule, if you can also comply with the solicitors' rule. You must comply with both, which will mean meeting the stricter standard. However, 15.01(4) addresses the possibility of a conflict of rules by disapplying any provisions of the solicitors' rules to the extent (and no more) that it conflicts with an applicable local rule. In a situation where compliance with both rules might be possible but perhaps create a bizarre result, application can be made to the SRA for a waiver.

10. Rule 15 modifies the provisions of other rules to allow for adaptation to the legal and professional framework of the jurisdiction in which you are practising. Sometimes more general provisions are substituted, in recognition of the fact that legal and market conditions may be very different in other jurisdictions.

11. Where a rule relates closely to the legal or regulatory framework in England and Wales it may be disapplied by rule 15 without a substitute. If a rule applies in part – for example rule 3 (Conflict of interests) – or in full – for example rule 4 (Confidentiality and disclosure), you will need to refer to that rule and its guidance, as well as the provisions in rule 15 and this guidance. Even if rule 15 has completely replaced the provisions of another rule, the guidance on the corresponding rule may help you to understand how you are expected to act.

Deposit interest – 15.15

20. In relation to overseas practice, you are not bound by the interest requirements in the Solicitors' Accounts Rules 1998, but by those in 15.15. You must ensure that a client gets proper interest – but this is subject to the proviso that the circumstances must be such that interest ought, in fairness, to be earned for the client. This might not be so if the interest is or would be negligible, or it is customary in that jurisdiction to deal with interest in a different way. It is also open to you to enter into a written agreement with the client regarding the payment of interest.

Accounts – 15.27

26. In relation to overseas practice, you are not bound by the Solicitors' Accounts Rules 1998 but by 15.27, which imposes similar but more general provisions. If an applicable local rule conflicts with a provision of 15.27, you will still be expected to comply with any other provisions of 15.27 that do not conflict.

27 Although the Solicitors' Accounts Rules 1998 do not apply, they may provide useful information about keeping accounts, the kind of checks an accountant might make, and the preparation of accountants' reports. Also, if your firm has offices in and outside England and Wales, a single accountant's report may be submitted covering your practice from offices both in, and outside, England and Wales – such a report must cover compliance both with the Solicitors' Accounts Rules 1998 and rule 15.27(3) of the Solicitors' Code of Conduct 2007.

28. The accounting requirements and the obligation to deliver an accountant's report in 15.27 are designed to apply to you in relation to money held or received by your firm unless it is primarily the practice of lawyers of other jurisdictions. The fact that they do not apply in certain cases is not intended to allow a lower standard of care in the handling of client money – simply

to prevent the Solicitors' Accounts Rules 1998 applying "by the back door" in a disproportionate or inappropriate way.

Rights and obligations of practice

20.06 Reporting serious misconduct and serious financial difficulty

You must (subject, where necessary, to your client's consent) report to the Solicitors Regulation Authority if:

(a) you become aware of serious misconduct by a solicitor, an REL, an RFL, a recognised body, a manager of a recognised body, or an employee of a recognised body or recognised sole practitioner;

(b) you have reason to doubt the integrity of a solicitor, an REL or an RFL, a manager of a recognised body or an employee of a recognised body or recognised sole practitioner; or

(c) you have reason to believe that a solicitor, an REL, an RFL, a recognised body, a manager of a recognised body, or a firm is in serious financial difficulty which could put the public at risk.

20.08 Production of documents, information and explanations

(1) You must promptly comply with:

(a) a written notice from the Solicitors Regulation Authority that you must produce for inspection by the appointee of the Solicitors Regulation Authority all documents held by you or held under your control and all information and explanations requested:

(i) in connection with your practice; or

(ii) in connection with any trust of which you are, or formerly were, a trustee;

for the purpose of ascertaining whether any person subject to these rules is complying with or has complied with any provision of these or any other rules, codes or mandatory guidance made or issued by the Solicitors Regulation Authority; and

(b) a notice given by the Solicitors Regulation Authority in accordance with section 44B or 44BA of the Solicitors Act 1974 for the provision of documents, information or explanations.

(2) You must provide any necessary permissions for information to be given so as to enable the appointee of the Solicitors Regulation Authority to:

(a) prepare a report on the documents produced under (1) above; and

(b) seek verification from clients, staff and the banks, building societies or other financial institutions used by you.

(3) You must comply with all requests from the Solicitors Regulation Authority or its appointee as to:

(a) the form in which you produce any documents you hold electronically; and

(b) photocopies of any documents to take away.

(4) A notice under this rule is deemed to be duly served:

(a) on the date on which it is delivered to or left at your address;

(b) on the date on which it is sent electronically to your e-mail or fax address; or

(c) seven days after it has been sent by post or document exchange to your last notified practising address.

Guidance to rule 20

Retirement from practice

19. You may continue to need a practising certificate after you retire, depending on how complete your retirement is. If you have closed your firm, but will continue to hold money for clients only while you submit bills of costs and close your practice accounts, you will still be subject to the Solicitors' Accounts Rules 1998. However, if that is all you are doing you will not need a practising certificate, provided that a solicitor with a practising certificate authorises any withdrawals from your client account.

...

Reporting serious misconduct and serious financial difficulty – 20.06

33. The purpose of 20.06 is to protect the public and the integrity of the profession. Often, professional colleagues will be aware of serious misconduct and/or risk arising from a firm's financial problems before any complaint has been made, and if the SRA is notified it can take timely action. The SRA's Fraud and Confidential Intelligence Bureau will consider information of this nature on an anonymous basis if requested.

34. Unless you are required by law to report a matter, 20.06 does not apply to confidential and/or privileged information another lawyer discloses to you:

(a) as your client or the client of your firm; or

(b) when seeking advice from a confidential helpline, such as the Solicitors' Assistance Scheme or Lawcare.

35. You will not breach 20.06 if you take no action because you know that someone else has already reported a matter of which you are aware.

36. Whether or not "misconduct" can be considered "serious", and whether or not a firm's financial difficulties could put the public at risk, will depend on

the circumstances. In general, any conduct involving dishonesty or deception or a serious criminal offence would amount to "serious misconduct". If in your judgement a firm's financial difficulties present a risk to its clients or to others, you should report the matter, and can do so on a confidential basis if you wish.

37. If reporting misconduct which has taken place within your own firm and which may give rise to a claim, you should also consider your obligations to your insurers. See also note 54 of the guidance to rule 3 (Conflict of interests).

38. If making a report about another lawyer or firm would involve disclosing confidential information, you should obtain your client's consent before proceeding.

39. You should exercise care where there may be evidence of money laundering activities (see the Proceeds of Crime Act 2002, other relevant statutes and regulations, and guidance issued by the Law Society and the SRA on this subject).

Production of documents, information and explanations – 20.08

42. The SRA will only exercise its powers under 20.08 in accordance with the law, in pursuit of a legitimate aim and proportionate to that aim.

43. The SRA may use or disclose any information obtained under 20.08 and the report prepared by its appointee:

(a) in proceedings before the Solicitors Disciplinary Tribunal;

(b) to the police, the Crown Prosecution Service or the Serious Fraud Office for use in investigating the matter and in any subsequent prosecution, if it appears that you or any manager, employee, member or owner of your firm may have committed a serious criminal offence;

(c) to your regulatory body in your home state or states if you are an REL or RFL;

(d) to the regulatory body with which you are registered, if you are a solicitor registered under the Establishment Directive;

(e) to the regulatory body of any manager or employee of your firm; and/or

(f) to the professional body of which the accountant who has signed the firm's accountant's report is a member, or by which the accountant is regulated (and the information and report may also be taken into account by the SRA in relation to a possible disqualification of that person from signing an accountant's report in future).

44. Note that sections 44B and 44BA of the Solicitors Act 1974 give the SRA power to require the production of documents, give information and to

provide explanations for the purpose of investigation whether there has been professional misconduct or regulatory non-compliance.

In-house solicitors

55. If you are an in-house solicitor, you do not have to hold a practising certificate unless:

    ...

    (e) you authorise the withdrawal of money from a client account, under rule 23(1)(a) of the Solicitors' Accounts Rules 1998.

Waivers

22.01

(1) In any particular case or cases the Solicitors Regulation Authority Board shall have power to waive in writing the provisions of these rules for a particular purpose or purposes expressed in such waiver, to place conditions on and to revoke such waiver.

Interpretation

24.01

In these rules, unless the context otherwise requires, all references to legislation include existing and future amendments to that legislation and:

"approved regulator" means a body listed in paragraph 1 of Schedule 4 to the Legal Services Act 2007 (whether or not that paragraph has been brought into force), or designated as an approved regulator by an order under paragraph 17 of that Schedule, and reference to the Solicitors Regulation Authority as an approved regulator means the Solicitors Regulation Authority carrying out regulatory functions assigned to the Law Society as an approved regulator;

    ...

"authorised non-SRA firm" means a sole practitioner, partnership, LLP or company authorised to practise by another approved regulator and not by the Solicitors Regulation Authority;

"body corporate" means:

    (a) a company;

    (b) an LLP; or

    (c) a partnership which is a legal person in its own right;

    ...

"client account" in rule 15 (Overseas practice), means an account at a bank or similar institution, subject to supervision by a public authority, which is used only for the purpose of holding client money and/or trust money, and the title or designation of which indicates that the funds in the account belong to the client or clients of a solicitor or REL or are held subject to a trust;

(for the definition of "client account" in relation to practice from an office in England and Wales, see the Solicitors' Accounts Rules 1998);

"client money" in rule 15 (Overseas practice), means money you receive or hold for or on behalf of a client or trust;

(for the definition of "client money" in relation to practice from an office in England and Wales, see the Solicitors' Accounts Rules 1998);

...

"director" means a director of a company, and includes the director of a recognised body which is a company; and in relation to a societas Europaea includes:

(a) in a two-tier system, a member of the management organ and a member of the supervisory organ; and

(b) in a one-tier system, a member of the administrative organ;

...

"employee" except in rule 6 (Equality and diversity) includes an individual who is:

(a) employed as a director of a company;

(b) engaged under a contract of service (for example, as an assistant solicitor) by a firm or its wholly owned service company; or

(c) engaged under a contract for services (for example, as a consultant or a locum), made between a firm or organisation and:

(i) that individual;

(ii) an employment agency; or

(iii) a company which is not held out to the public as providing legal services and is wholly owned and directed by that individual,

under which the firm or organisation has exclusive control over the individual's time for all or part of the individual's working week; or in relation to which the firm or organisation has designated the individual as a fee earner in accordance with arrangements between the firm or organisation and the Legal Services Commission pursuant to the Access to Justice Act 1999;

and "employer" and "employment" must be construed accordingly;

"Establishment Directive" means the Establishment of Lawyers Directive 98/5/EC;

"Establishment Directive profession" means any profession listed in Article 1.2(a) of the Establishment Directive, including a solicitor, barrister or advocate of the UK;

"Establishment Directive Regulations" means the European Communities (Lawyer's Practice) Regulations 2000 (SI 2000/1119);

"Establishment Directive state" means a state to which the Establishment of Lawyers Directive 98/5/EC applies – currently all the states of the EU plus Iceland, Liechtenstein, Norway and Switzerland;

...

"firm" means any business through which a solicitor or REL carries on practice other than in-house practice;

"foreign lawyer" means a person who is not a solicitor or barrister of England and Wales, but who is a member, and entitled to practise as such, of a legal profession regulated within a jurisdiction outside England and Wales;

...

"in-house practice" means a solicitor's practice within 12.01(1)(e) or 12.01(2)(e), or an REL's practice within 12.02(1)(e) or 12.02(2)(e);

"lawyer" means a member of one of the following professions, entitled to practise as such:

(a) the profession of solicitor, barrister or advocate of the UK;

(b) a profession whose members are authorised to practise by an approved regulator other than the Solicitors Regulation Authority;

(c) an Establishment Directive profession other than a UK profession;

(d) a legal profession which has been approved by the Solicitors Regulation Authority for the purpose of recognised bodies in England and Wales; or

(e) any other regulated legal profession which is recognised as such by the Solicitors Regulation Authority;

"lawyer of England and Wales" means a solicitor with a current practising certificate or an individual who is authorised to practise in England and Wales by an approved regulator other than the Solicitors Regulation Authority, but excludes a member of an Establishment Directive profession registered with the Bar Standards Board under the Establishment Directive;

"legal profession" means a profession whose members are lawyers as defined in this rule;

"legally qualified body" for the purposes of these rules and for the purposes of section 9A(6)(h) and (6C) of the Administration of Justice Act 1985 means a body which would meet the services requirement in 14.01(1) and is:

(a) a recognised body;

(b) an authorised non-SRA firm of which individuals who are, and are entitled to practise as, lawyers of England and Wales, lawyers of Establishment Directive professions or RFLs make up at least 75% of the ultimate beneficial ownership; or

(c) a European corporate practice;

"LLP" means a limited liability partnership formed by being incorporated under the Limited Liability Partnerships Act 2000;

"manager" means:

    (a)   a partner in a partnership;

    (b)   a member of an LLP; or

    (c)   a director of a company;

"member" in relation to a recognised body, means:

    (a)   a person who has agreed to be a member of a company and whose name is entered in the company's register of members; or

    (b)   a member of an LLP;

"non-lawyer" means:

    (a)   an individual who is not a lawyer practising as such; or

    (b)   a body corporate or partnership which is not:

        (i)   a recognised body;

        (ii)   an authorised non-SRA firm; or

        (iii)   a business, carrying on the practice of lawyers from an office or offices outside England and Wales, in which a controlling majority of the owners and managers are lawyers;

...

"overseas" means in or of a jurisdiction other than England and Wales;

"overseas practice" means:

    (a)   the practice from an office outside England and Wales of:

        (i)   a solicitor;

        (ii)   a recognised body;

        (iii)   a manager of a recognised body who is a lawyer of England and Wales;

    (b)   the activities of an individual non-lawyer as a manager of a recognised body practising from an office outside England and Wales;

    (c)   the activities of a body corporate as a manager of a recognised body practising from an office outside England and Wales; and

    (d)   the practice of an REL from an office in Scotland or Northern Ireland;

"owner" in relation to a body, means a person with any ownership interest in the body;

"partner" means a person who is or is held out as a partner in an unincorporated firm;

"partnership" means an unincorporated partnership, and includes any un-incorporated firm in which persons are or are held out as partners, but does not include an LLP;

"person" includes an individual and a body corporate;

...

"practice" means:

(a) the activities of a solicitor, in that capacity;

(b) (i) the activities of an REL in the capacity of lawyer of an Establishment Directive profession, from an office or offices within the UK; or

(ii) the activities of a member of an Establishment Directive profession registered with the Bar Standards Board under the Establishment Directive, in that capacity, from an office or offices in the UK;

(c) the activities of an RFL from an office or offices in England and Wales as:

(i) the employee of a recognised sole practitioner;

(ii) a manager, employee, member or owner of a recognised body or of an authorised non-SRA firm;

(iii) a manager, member or owner of a body corporate which is a manager, member or owner of a recognised body or of an authorised non-SRA firm;

(d) the activities of a recognised body;

(e) the activities of an individual non-lawyer:

(i) as a manager of a recognised body; or

(ii) employed in England and Wales by a recognised body or recognised sole practitioner;

(f) the activities of a body corporate as a manager of a recognised body;

(g) the activities of a lawyer of England and Wales, in that capacity; and

(h) the activities of an authorised non-SRA firm,

and "practise" and "practising" should be construed accordingly;

"practice from an office" includes practice carried on:

(a) from an office at which you are based; or

(b) from an office of a firm in which you are the sole principal, or a manager, or in which you have an ownership interest, even if you are not based there,

and "practising from an office in England and Wales", etc. should be construed accordingly;

"practice through a body" includes having an ownership interest in a body and being a director if the body is a company, even if you yourself undertake no work for the body's clients, and "practising through an authorised non-SRA firm" should be construed accordingly;

"principal" means a sole practitioner or a partner in a partnership;

...

"Recognised Bodies Regulations" means the SRA Recognised Bodies Regulations 2009;

"recognised body" means a partnership, company or LLP for the time being recognised by the Solicitors Regulation Authority under section 9 of the Administration of Justice Act 1985 and the Recognised Bodies Regulations;

"recognised sole practitioner" means a solicitor or REL authorised by the Solicitors Regulation Authority under section 1B of the Solicitors Act 1974 to practise as a sole practitioner;

...

"REL (registered European lawyer)" means an individual registered with the Solicitors Regulation Authority under regulation 17 of the Establishment Directive Regulations;

"REL-controlled recognised body" means a recognised body in which RELs, or RELs together with lawyers of England and Wales and/or European lawyers registered with the Bar Standards Board, constitute the national group of lawyers with the largest (or equal largest) share of control of the recognised body either as individual managers or by their share in the control of bodies which are managers, and for this purpose RELs and European lawyers registered with the Bar Standards Board belong to the national group of England and Wales;

...

"RFL (registered foreign lawyer)" means an individual registered with the Solicitors Regulation Authority under section 89 of the Courts and Legal Services Act 1990;

...

"societas Europaea" means a European public limited liability company within the meaning of article 1 of Council Regulation 2157/2001/EC;

"sole practitioner" means a solicitor or REL practising as a sole principal, and does not include a solicitor or REL practising in-house;

"solicitor-controlled recognised body" means a recognised body in which lawyers of England and Wales constitute the national group of lawyers with the largest (or equal largest) share of control of the recognised body either as individual managers or by their share in the control of bodies which are managers;

...

"UK" means United Kingdom;

Part 3

Annexes

[with consolidated amendments to 31 March 2009]

A. Solicitors Act 1974, ss.34, 34A, 34B and 85

34. Accountants' reports

(1) The Society may make rules requiring solicitors to provide the Society with reports signed by an accountant (in this section referred to as an "accountant's report") at such times or in such circumstances as may be prescribed by the rules.

(2) The rules may specify requirements to be met by, or in relation to, an accountant's report (including requirements relating to the accountant who signs the report).

(3)–(5A) [repealed]

(6) If any solicitor fails to comply with the provisions of any rules made under this section, a complaint in respect of that failure may be made to the Tribunal by or on behalf of the Society.

(7)–(8) [repealed]

(9) Where an accountant, during the course of preparing an accountant's report –

   (a) discovers evidence of fraud or theft in relation to money held by a solicitor for a client or any other person (including money held on trust) or money held in an account of a client of a solicitor, or an account of another person, which is operated by the solicitor, or

   (b) obtains information which the accountant has reasonable cause to believe is likely to be of material significance in determining whether a solicitor is a fit and proper person to hold money for clients or other persons (including money held on trust) or to operate an account of a client of the solicitor or an account of another person,

   the accountant must immediately give a report of the matter to the Society.

(10) No duty to which an accountant is subject is to be regarded as contravened merely because of any information or opinion contained in a report under subsection (9).

34A Employees of solicitors

(1) Rules made by the Society may provide for any rules made under section 31, 32, 33A or 34 to have effect in relation to employees of solicitors with such additions, omissions or other modifications as appear to the Society to be necessary or expedient.

(2) If any employee of a solicitor fails to comply with rules made under section 31 or 32, as they have effect in relation to the employee by virtue of subsection (1), any person may make a complaint in respect of that failure to the Tribunal.

(3) If any employee of a solicitor fails to comply with rules made under section 34, as they have effect in relation to the employee by virtue of subsection (1), a complaint in respect of that failure may be made to the Tribunal by or on behalf of the Society.

34B Employees of solicitors: accounts rules etc

(1) Where rules made under section 32(1) have effect in relation to employees of solicitors by virtue of section 34A(1), section 85 applies in relation to an employee to whom the rules have effect who keeps an account with a bank or building society in pursuance of such rules as it applies in relation to a solicitor who keeps such an account in pursuance of rules under section 32.

(2) Subsection (3) applies where rules made under section 32 –

    (a) contain any such provision as is referred to in section 33(1), and

    (b) have effect in relation to employees of solicitors by virtue of section 34A(1).

(3) Except as provided by the rules, an employee to whom the rules are applied is not liable to account to any client, other person or trust for interest received by the employee on money held at a bank or building society in an account which is for money received or held for, or on account of –

    (a) clients of the solicitor, other persons or trusts, generally, or

    (b) that client, person or trust, separately.

(4) Subsection (5) applies where rules made under section 33A(1) have effect in relation to employees of solicitors by virtue of section 34A(1).

(5) The Society may disclose a report on or information about the accounts of any employee of a solicitor obtained in pursuance of such rules for use –

    (a) in investigating the possible commission of an offence by the solicitor or any employees of the solicitor, and

    (b) in connection with any prosecution of the solicitor or any employees of the solicitor consequent on the investigation.

(6) Where rules made under section 34 have effect in relation to employees of solicitors by virtue of section 34A(1), section 34(9) and (10) apply in relation to such an employee as they apply in relation to a solicitor.

85. Bank accounts

Where a solicitor keeps an account with a bank or building society in pursuance of rules under section 32 –

(a) the bank or society shall not incur any liability, or be under any obligation to make any inquiry, or be deemed to have any knowledge of any right of any person to any money paid or credited to the account, which it would not incur or be under or be deemed to have in the case of an account kept by a person entitled absolutely to all the money paid or credited to it; and

(b) the bank or society shall not have any recourse or right against money standing to the credit of the account, in respect of any liability of the solicitor to the bank or society, other than a liability in connection with the account.

B. Treatment of VAT on counsel's fees – practice information

This note sets out the concessionary treatment for counsel's fees paid into and kept in client account agreed between HM Revenue and Customs (HMRC) and the Law Society at the time VAT was first introduced, in 1973.

There are two ways in which you may treat counsel's fees:

Method (i)

You may treat the fee as your own expense and thus reclaim the VAT element as input tax. When you deliver your own bill of costs to your client, the value of the supply for VAT purposes is the value of your own costs, plus the tax *exclusive* value of counsel's fees.

Example

Assume your professional charges are £1,200 plus £210 VAT (assuming a rate of 17.5%), and the bill includes unpaid counsel's fees of £800, plus £140 VAT. The £140 VAT on counsel's fee note is treated as your input tax and can be reclaimed by you from HMRC. Your bill should show:

Legal services	£1,200.00	
Counsel's fees	£800.00	
		£2,000.00
VAT @ 17.5%		£350.00
TOTAL		£2,350.00

When payment of £2,350 is received, the accounts rules[1] provide that the sum of £2,350 may either:

•   be paid into an office account at a bank or building society in England and Wales; by the end of the second working day following receipt, the amount due to counsel of £940 (£800 plus VAT of £140) must either be paid out of office account or be transferred to client account pending payment; or

- be split between client account and office account as appropriate, or be paid into client account with a transfer out of client account of office monies (£1,200 costs and £350 VAT) within 14 days of receipt.

Because counsel's fee is being treated for VAT purposes as an expense of the solicitor and the VAT element is being reclaimed by you, payment, when it is made, must be from office account (so that the appropriate entry can be made in the VAT ledger account). At that stage the sum held in client account can be transferred to office account.

Note

1.   Rules 19(1)(b) and 20 – the option in rule 19(1)(b) may be used only if the payment includes no client money other than professional disbursements incurred but not yet paid.

Method (ii)

You may treat counsel's advice as supplied directly to your client and the settlement of the fees as a disbursement for VAT purposes. Counsel's VAT invoice (receipted fee note) may be amended by

- inserting on the fee note your client's name and the word "per" immediately preceding your own name and address; or

- crossing out your name and address and replacing it with the name and address of your client.

The fee note from counsel will then be recognised as a valid VAT invoice in the hands of your client (who can reclaim the VAT if registered) and no VAT record need be kept in your accounts ledgers. You should keep a photocopy of the VAT invoice.

Where you consider that the services of counsel, if supplied directly to the client, would be outside the scope of UK VAT, you must *not* certify counsel's fee note to this effect and pay counsel only the fee net of VAT. You may advise counsel that VAT is not due on their services because of the place of belonging of the client. You may provide them with appropriate commercial evidence of the client's place of belonging. Where the client is in business in other EC Member States, this evidence could be the client's EU VAT registration number, but if no EU VAT number is provided and the client is in business in the EU, counsel should obtain commercial evidence to this effect. A statement from you that the client is in business would not be sufficient. Where the client belongs outside the EU and Isle of Man, counsel should obtain commercial evidence to confirm the place of belonging. Where no evidence of belonging is obtained, counsel should charge VAT on their services.

Example

Assuming the same level of professional charges and counsel's fees as above, your bill should show:

Legal services	£1,200.00
VAT @ 17.5%	£210.00
	£1,410.00
Counsel's fees (including VAT)	£940.00
TOTAL	£2,350.00

If the intention is to take advantage of the concessionary treatment and treat the supply as being made direct to your client, payment of counsel's fees must not be made from office account. The option in rule 19(1)(b) of paying into office account, and then either paying counsel or transferring the amount due to client account pending payment, cannot therefore be used.

When payment is received from your client, the cheque must either be split as to £1,410 office account and £940 client account, or alternatively the entire sum of £2,350 must be paid into client account with a transfer out of the office monies within 14 days of receipt.

Revised May 2009

C. US limited liability partnerships

1. Purpose of this note

This note looks at US limited liability partnerships (LLPs) and how the Accounts Rules and the Code of Conduct affect solicitors who are partners in a US LLP.

2. The nature of US LLPs

Prior to 31 March 2009 the SRA had to distinguish for regulatory purposes between three different types of US LLP:

- an LLP which (like an English general partnership) has no separate legal personality and is simply a collection of partners carrying on business together – e.g. LLPs formed under the laws of New York State, Illinois and Georgia: "category A" LLPs;

- an LLP which has separate legal personality – e.g. LLPs formed under the laws of California, Texas, Minnesota and Washington DC: "category B" LLPs;

- an LLP which has separate legal personality but whose partners can exercise the option to negative that separate legal personality – LLPs formed under Delaware law: "category C" LLPs.

3. US LLP: practice as a recognised body in England and Wales

Before 31 March 2009, a partnership with separate legal personality committed a criminal offence under the Solicitors Act 1974 if it had an English solicitor partner and practised in England and Wales. This prevented "category B" LLPs from practising in England and Wales if they had any English solicitor partners. The same applied to a "category C" LLP with separate legal personality.

As from 31 March 2009 any US LLP with an English solicitor partner may now practise in England and Wales, provided it first obtains recognition from the SRA as a "recognised body" under section 9 of the Administration of Justice Act 1985.

Note that a US LLP is not an LLP as defined in the Solicitors' Code of Conduct 2007, the Solicitors' Accounts Rules 1998 or the Solicitors' Indemnity Insurance Rules. The rules that apply to it will be the rules applying to a partnership.

Notepaper of a US LLP practising as a recognised body in England/Wales

A US LLP which is a recognised body must have on its English notepaper a statement that it is regulated by the Solicitors Regulation Authority.

The notepaper must identify the state law under which the limited liability partnership is formed.

If there are 20 or fewer partners, the US LLP's notepaper must carry a list of the partners. If the US LLP has more than 20 partners, the notepaper must carry either a list of the partners or a statement that a list of partners is open to inspection at the office. In all cases the list must give the qualifications of all the partners:

- identifying solicitors as such;

- identifying US lawyers as US lawyers or attorneys, or naming the states in which they are qualified;

- identifying other foreign lawyers in terms of their country of qualification – and in the case of European lawyers their professional qualification in the language of their home jurisdiction;

- where practising with other English lawyers (barristers, legal executives, etc.), identifying them in terms of the profession concerned;

- where practising with non-lawyers, identifying them as non-lawyers or non-lawyer partners;

- where practising with one or more corporate partners, identifying the nature of that corporate partner if this is not clear from its name.

Compulsory professional indemnity insurance

Under the Solicitors' Indemnity Insurance Rules the US LLP must have "qualifying insurance" with a "qualifying insurer" of at least £2 million for any one claim in respect of practice carried on from the firm's office or offices in England and Wales. The only exception is that if the firm's partners include a limited company or LLP, the minimum cover required will be £3 million.

Accounts and accountant's reports

Accounts in respect of the practice of the office or offices in England and Wales must be maintained in accordance with the Solicitors' Accounts Rules 1998. Client money must be kept in a client account of the firm at a branch (or head office) in England and Wales of a bank or building society as defined in the rules. There are limited exceptions to this rule. An accountant's report on the firm's dealings with client money must be delivered to the SRA every year.

4. US LLP: overseas branch of a recognised body

Compulsory professional indemnity insurance

If the recognised body has a branch office outside England and Wales, the Solicitors' Indemnity Insurance Rules do not apply to that office. Instead, rule 15.26 of the Code of Conduct requires solicitor partners and employees to have reasonable indemnity cover. The rule will not apply to the recognised body itself unless it is a "solicitor-controlled" recognised body.

Accounts and accountant's reports

If the recognised body has a branch office outside England and Wales, the Solicitors' Accounts Rules 1998 do not apply to that office. Accounts in respect of the recognised body's office or offices outside England and Wales will have to be maintained, and annual accountant's reports delivered, in accordance with rule 15.27 of the Code of Conduct, but only if the firm is a "solicitor-controlled" recognised body. If any solicitor partner or employee holds client money as a named trustee, accounts must be maintained and reports delivered in respect of that money, even if the firm is not a "solicitor-controlled" recognised body.

5. US LLP with no offices in England and Wales

This paragraph looks at solicitors practising as partners or employees of a US LLP with no branch offices in England and Wales. (This could be the "parent" firm which is associated with a US LLP practising as a recognised body in England and Wales.)

Compulsory professional indemnity insurance

Rule 15.26 of the Code of Conduct requires solicitor partners and employees to have reasonable indemnity cover.

Accounts and accountant's reports

Rule 15.27 of the Code of Conduct (accounts and accountant's reports for overseas offices) will not apply unless the firm is controlled by solicitors; except that if any solicitor partner or employee holds client money as a named trustee, accounts must be maintained and reports delivered in respect of that money, even if the firm is not controlled by solicitors.

D Tax on bank and building society interest – HMRC guidance

[from *Business Income Manual* (BIM65805) as amended on 24 October 2005]

Bank and building society interest on deposits of clients' money should be dealt with as follows:

(a) Designated clients' deposit account. The client is entitled to the interest arising on the account and depending upon the status of the client the interest may be paid gross or net. The solicitor will simply pass on the interest gross or net to the client.

(b) Undesignated deposit accounts. Deduction of tax does not apply to interest on an undesignated (general) client account.

Where money is deposited into an undesignated client account the interest arises to the solicitor and is chargeable on him under Case III. At the same time the solicitor owes his clients an amount corresponding to the funds deposited, and will account to each client for interest thereon. Interest paid by the solicitor is chargeable on the client under Case III. The solicitor will be required to deduct tax only if ICTA88/S349 (2)(c) applies, i.e. where the interest is both "yearly", and paid to a client whose usual place of abode is overseas.

The solicitor is to be assessed under Case III only on the net interest retained in the year. Where the amount paid to clients exceeds the interest received the excess may be allowed as a Case II deduction.

The tax treatment of the interest in the hands of the client is explained at IM1508.